START JOURNALING TODAY

WHAT YOU NEED TO TRY THIS OUT FOR YOURSELF

JESS MAPLE

© Copyright 2021 - All rights reserved.

It is not legal to reproduce, duplicate, or transmit any part of this document in either electronic means or in printed format. Recording of this publication is strictly prohibited and any storage of this document is not allowed unless with written permission from the publisher except for the use of brief quotations in a book review.

CONTENTS

How To Use This Book   v

1. Introduction: What Is Journaling?   1
2. What Do I Need? Equipment   13
3. What Do I Need? A Place Where I Can Journal   29
4. Where Do I Start? Start Here   41
5. Carving Out Space In Your Day   51
6. First Steps In Writing To Yourself   59
7. Writing A Little Every Day   71
8. Stop! Writing Things Down When Your Mind Is Busy   89
9. Habits: Forming Them And Keeping Them   109
10. Next Steps   125

Appendix   131
References   135

HOW TO USE THIS BOOK

Welcome. This book is jam packed with journaling ideas for you to try out for yourself. Please think of this book as a deluxe menu to choose from rather than a complete list of everything that you need to do. With that in mind, here are some recommended places to start.

- Start at **Chapter 1** if you want to know about the idea of journaling and the equipment you might want or need to get started.
- Start at **Chapter 4** if you want to start writing straight away and then learn more later.
- Start with **Chapter 8** if you want to learn how to clear your mind of busy thoughts first, before learning about other ways to journal. This is a standalone chapter—and then you can return to this menu to decide on your next steps.

This book is designed to be read slowly, perhaps a chapter at a time. Each chapter will give you some things to try out before moving onto the next chapter. It is as important, if not more important, that you take action, try out some of the exercises and see which you prefer—before learning more in the next chapter.

SOME HELP WITH TIMING

- Spend however long you need at Chapter 4, trying some odd bits of writing, before making decisions about how to add this into your routine (Chapter 5).
- Spend a few weeks at Chapter 6 trying this out more regularly and reflecting on each week before progressing to Chapter 7.
- Spend up to 3 months journaling using ideas from across Chapters 3 to 7 (whatever is working for you) before reflecting on how it is going and reading Chapter 9 for more insights.
- After 6 months to a year, you might want to try one of our other books.

INTRODUCTION: WHAT IS JOURNALING?

"Your Journal is like your best friend. You don't have to pretend with it, you can be honest and write exactly how you feel."

— BUKOLA OGUNWALE

Life is a collection of experiences, and as we go through its ups and downs, we keep a lot of things in our heads—our hopes and dreams, plans and to-do lists, successes and failures, our feelings at particular moments, secrets, and so on.

Some of these things we are very aware of, some painfully so. Others, we don't tend to think about or focus on day to day.

What was it like the first time you met your romantic partner? What do you worry about when you are lying in bed trying to get to sleep? What were your dreams and aspirations 5 years ago compared to now? What's the most important message you convey to your children the next time they mess up?

Journaling provides you with a way to pay more attention to your thoughts, feelings, memories, aspirations, values, and so on—and make sense of them by transferring them from your mind to paper.

Journaling opens an avenue for you to reflect upon your life and take stock of your progress. It gives you detailed reference points on the events in your life; not just when they happened, but also what you thought about them at the time—your thought process prior to changing jobs, the relationships that you truly valued two years ago, the dreams and aspirations of your career that made so much sense, how they evolved over time and what inspired any changes.

It allows you to learn as much as you can from your past in order to help you create the kind of life that suits you as an individual—and sculpt your future. It also helps you connect more to events as they are happening, choose how you wish to be involved and make better decisions as you are going along on your journey.

A journal does not have to be just a repository of memories for reference and timestamps of life events. It can be so much more, and the beauty of it is that you can make it whatever it needs to be for you. No rules, no restrictions, but an important ritual that helps you connect to your inner self, for you and yourself only.

Some people picked up journaling as a habit quite young in life and literally have an on-paper documentary of nearly every day they have lived in this world: the quirks and nonsense of childhood, prepubescent desires, teenage relationships, ambitions, and how they constructed their worldview as they went along. This could make for a riveting if not an embarrassing read in your mid-twenties, but definitely a worthwhile insight into who you were when life was less complicated (or potentially more complicated depending on your adolescence!).

You might know someone who started this valuable method of processing life in middle or high school, and might have noticed that they carried themselves differently to you. They perhaps seemed calmer and more confident, more able to express what was important to them or got along better with other people than you did.

Journaling has been proven to help you achieve greater self-awareness, which adds richness to your life, as well as helping you find solutions to day-to-day-problems such as worries, sleep, and tricky decisions. To say the least, journaling is a healthy habit that everyone can benefit from.

For some perspective, take a look at a few excerpts showing what teenagers who responded to a BuzzFeed survey felt about journaling (Miller, 2017).

- *"My diary really helps me feel normal and helps me feel like the good days are always going to come."*
- *"Writing in my journal forces me to notice things more, which gives me time to breathe and practice awareness, somehow slowing the time down."*
- *"I guess it's best described as the mess in my head is like a huge knot of yarn. When I write, it's like untangling that knot and being able to see the whole string laid out."*

Even if you might not have already made journaling a habit, it won't be a completely alien concept. Most people are already familiar with the term "diary," which is a similar concept to "journal" but let me walk you through the differences below.

IS A DIARY A JOURNAL?

A diary is defined as *a book in which one keeps a daily record of events and experiences*. You can also use one to plan for future dates such as mapping out important dates and meetings to keep organized, or track personal data such as exercise, diet, weight or mood in a structured way.

You would mainly use a diary to note down things you do not want to forget—activities of the day, what was completed and what needs completing. One of the most famous diaries is Anne Frank's—a German-Dutch Jew who was a victim of the Holocaust. It was published as a book titled *The Diary of a Young Girl*, translated into over 70 languages, and the subject of several films and plays.

Trapped in Amsterdam after the German occupation of the Netherlands, Anne wrote regularly in her diary of her daily experiences and future dreams for about two years until her family was captured in August 1944, when she was only 15 years old.

While a journal can share the same meaning as a diary, it is much more than that. It also refers to a newspaper or other publication that deals with a specific profession or subject, for example, *The Wall Street Journal* or *The International Journal of Psychology*. There are many other *journals* that are not necessarily *diaries* and not at all personal, such as a nautical journal that details the movements of a ship on its voyage.

Fun fact: While both will often always mean exactly the same thing, a journal can mean much more. According to Google's literature database, the word *diary* is used half as often as the word *journal*.

Away from the formal definitions, journals tend to be more personal, or "deeper" than diaries and incorporate emotions, problems and feelings, as well as plans of action and/or messages of self-assurance. They are not merely records of daily experiences and activities, but involve more active and intentional reflection, the practices of listening within, challenging yourself and letting yourself be vulnerable while exploring these topics.

The beauty of journaling is that it does not necessarily have to be a daily activity, which some would consider to be a chore—you can choose to journal only when you have significant experiences. You might also want to do it in short bursts for example for the month of which you are traveling or during summer vacation. It can take many forms and can typically include your interests, for example if you enjoy drawing you can draw freely in your journal as well as writing.

Another regular ritual is listing. For instance, you can have a regular gratitude list, a bucket list, a movie list, a travel list, an achievement list, a routine list, and so on. You can literally create any kind of list you can think of in a simple subformat called bullet journaling.

Due to its unstructured nature as compared to a diary, a journal allows you to create a way of working that suits you. It is ideal for creative ventures (a creative writing project, for example), but also recording notes on dreams, thoughts, travel, goals and ideas without having to follow a preordained format.

SO, SHOULD I CHOOSE A DIARY OR A JOURNAL?

With the above said, it doesn't really matter whether you are calling it a diary or journal, since in common usage both words are interchangeable. What matters is the purpose to which you are putting your regular writing.

To help you visualize this, let us explore what a *diary* and *journal* entry would look like if someone was writing about the same topic or theme in both formats.

- On fitness, a *diary* entry would be a record of your physical activity for the day, while a *journal* entry would be your experience working out, with things like notes on perfecting specific yoga poses, for instance.
- On career, a typical *diary* entry would comprise meeting dates, appointments, and completed tasks, while a typical *journal* entry would contain aspirations, dreams, and the big picture career goals.
- On nutrition, in a *diary* you'd put the food you had on that day and the derived feeling, while in a *journal* you would have notes on interesting recipes to try or your nutrition goals for the summer.

Now, it is not as black and white as it might seem from these examples, and I cannot emphasize enough that there are no rules in journaling. You are free to experiment, tweak and make it work for you and you alone. You might find some fancy styles used by others attractive, which is okay, just remember you are not trying to compete with anybody.

Straight answer: If you are strictly aiming at structured writing and being organized, a *diary* should be just fine—

tracking data can help you see useful links, such as between diet and migraines or mood and physical activity.

If you do not want to be confined, journaling is for you. It offers an experience of organic creativity without the constraints of calendar dates. You can freely jot down random ideas, doodles, lists, pictures, memories, anything crossing your mind no matter how short or long-lasting it is.

In practice, however, what matters is whether the format you have started with fits your needs. You will find this out over time, perhaps change some things up before understanding what works best for you. With consistent and regular practice, you will achieve what you set out to. A Royal College of Psychiatrists study (Baikie & Wilhelm, 2005) also found that expressive writing was associated with long-term physical and emotional well-being.

WHY JOURNALING?

Journaling is an instrument for emotional exploration, a free self-expression tool that promises personal growth and a creative outcome. When you put down your feelings and thoughts, you are by default compelled to take a step back and reflect on what is happening in your life rather than brushing it aside.

You can make it whatever you would want it to be for yourself. A gateway to recording your life as it unfolds and discovering things about yourself that you had never thought of. It would be naïve to assume that you already know all you need to know about yourself. Unrestrained private self-expression in writing will help you experience emotions you previously might not have been aware of and introduce you step by step to a more nuanced version of yourself.

It can, to a large extent, be a fun ritual especially when you are writing about the positive things that leave you all fuzzy and warm. You will be looking back at them in the future months and years to come with nostalgia.

But it can also be painful during the hard times: when we are overwhelmed by life, when our assumptions and beliefs are challenged, or when we would rather not confront the reality head-on. It is even more useful in such situations by nudging us to face discomfort rather than turning our backs away. It can also provide relief by offering us a place to write down what is stressing us out in the moment and making it more manageable when we choose to face it again later.

Instead of merely focusing on *what* happened, random journaling inherently allows you to go further, to explore the underlying effects and meanings. While venturing into the unfamiliar will often be associated with fear and discomfort, this is the natural way to growth and discovery—deeper self-awareness demands a willingness to be uncomfortable.

Journaling can be a brief moment in your day where you can escape all the heat that life gives, the noise and clutter of the everyday, and put your soul at rest. Given the fast-paced environment we live in, you are bound to at times feel that you are too mentally crowded or emotionally tired to really sit down and write. But deep down, you might crave some semblance of peace.

By journaling, you consciously give yourself the quiet you need to rebuild and regenerate. The still time that is yours alone; calming, restorative, and in a sense, healing.

IS JOURNALING FOR ME?

First, randomly pick any successful person in the world, anyone you deem successful by your own standards and try to find out if they keep or have kept a journal. Oprah? Einstein? Beyonce? Obama? Kamala Harris? Steve Jobs?

A sample Google search should look like this: "[person's name] + journaling." You will be surprised to find that many successful people practice some form of journaling.

Journaling is fairly simple and can be done by anyone with ease and without necessarily becoming an additional burden or chore to an already busy life. As we have emphasized earlier, the beauty is in customizing it for yourself. For instance, take a look at the simplicity of the below journaling rituals (Simmons, 2017).

- Benjamin Franklin would ask himself every morning, "*What good shall I do this day?*" to be clear on what was important to him at the start of each day. At the end of each day, he would ask himself "*What good have I done today?*" to reflect on whether he had met these goals and acted according to his values.
- Steve Jobs once said that every morning, he asked himself this question, "*If today were the last day of my life, would I want to do what I am about to do?*" to help him prioritize and focus on doing the things that were most important to him and society first. This also provided the motivation to start now and not put things off—procrastination—a problem that a lot of us have.
- Arianna Huffington and Oprah both start their day by filling their gratitude journals—noting down a

few things that they are thankful for. This boosts their mood at the beginning of their day and makes them then more likely to see the positives around them as they go about the rest of their day.

See? It doesn't have to be complex at all. Simple rituals like these can be as calming as they are focusing. If you choose to journal in the mornings as in the above examples, you will rarely (if ever) start your day with your mind in the wrong place.

There is no right or wrong way of journaling. You will even find yourself changing formats, from the written word, to doodling, drawing or painting. By all means keep it interesting, stay curious and go with the flow unhindered.

START HERE

This book is specifically designed for anyone who is interested in journaling and looking for an easy step-by-step guide to starting a potentially lifelong journey of self-exploration, growth and continually adding richness to their life. Don't worry about the rest of your life now, though. Just get started.

You do not need to have had any prior experience with journaling, because we got you covered. If you have already started with some form of journaling, this beginner book will help you get grounded on the basics that you may not have formally learned. It will help you to continue with this rewarding experience and maybe try some new things.

Unlike other resources that you may have tried, this book doesn't set out to make grand claims about what you can achieve with journaling: about completely changing your life, being the most successful person in the room or finding spiritual nirvana. We are about starting small and starting now. This is not to say that you don't have grand things in your future or you can't dream big, but to show you today, this week, this year, that small changes can make a significant difference and that there is value in everyday rituals.

Neither is this book going to attempt to make a medical diagnosis or treatment plan for you. There are numbers and websites for additional support in the appendix, which we hope are useful for those of you who may need them during difficult times.

Instead, this book offers you a toolkit that allows you the freedom to explore journaling and make it work for you and your life. Rather than stifling structure, or a requirement to fit in, this book acts like a guide or non-judgy friend that you can consult through this journey. We offer you the fundamentals, an array of choices, suggestions and exercises to try. You will be well equipped to try things out and experiment and then make decisions about how you want to journal moving forward. Your journaling could be blissful, sometimes painful and always useful.

The next nine chapters are going to delve deeper into what you need to get started; equipment and the ideal place, how to begin and the common blocks to writing, carving out time for this new habit, the first steps in writing for yourself, how to progress to writing a little every day, how to form and maintain your new habits, and the potential next steps available to you after learning the basics. There is also a standalone chapter on how to take swift action to relieve and declutter your mind when it is full as well as ways to reduce your worries in the longer term.

This is the first book in our ***Journaling Is for Everyone*** series which should give you a solid grounding in this habit that has been practiced by many people in the world, before you are invited to venture further into more advanced journaling or go deeper into a topic that interests you with another one of our books in the series.

We are also looking to build a community of like-minded people who are starting out on their journaling journey and would like to connect. If you are interested in joining this community, you can let us know at:

jessmaple@robinroundpress.com

This guide will occasionally draw from existing scientific literature as well as personal accounts of journalers who have experienced the full potential of consistently putting down their thoughts, feelings, ideas and projections on paper.

Yes, this is something that you are definitely capable of doing! In fact, as the title of this series of books assures us, "Journaling is for everyone."

Are you ready? Let's Begin!

2

WHAT DO I NEED? EQUIPMENT

One of the best pieces of advice you will ever get as a journaling beginner, and indeed when embarking on any potentially lifelong habit, is to start small. If you plunge yourself into the haste of getting every single accessory that is recommended in the initial stages, you might get overwhelmed and potentially lose sight of the very reason you wanted to start journaling.

Once you start journaling regularly and have found your style, you can gradually stock up on the accessories, get a little more fancy and even keep more than one journal at the same time.

If you feel like you already have enough equipment to get started, then by all means skip over the detail in this chapter and come back to it later for some more ideas.

PEN AND PAPER OR KEYBOARD AND SCREEN?

We recommend that you begin with an actual pen and paper journal as opposed to typing. This is because the physical act of writing has proven links with helping you target your intentions. Writing by hand encourages you to engage more deeply with what you are noting down, while typing can cause you to be disengaged or distracted.

That said, typing has its advantages as well, including the ability to create backups, accessing your journal on multiple devices on the go, and making it easier to retrieve specific entries.

There is also hybrid journaling using tools such as iPad and iPencil that sort of gives you the best of both worlds, combining the experience of free handwriting in a digital format.

Writing by hand is seen by many as gratifying, as it engages and stimulates your brain more, as well as helping you retain information. The more complex and subtle finger motions increase the activity in the motor cortex of your brain as a study published in the journal *Developmental Neuropsychology* (Berninger et al., 2006) found.

The researchers found that for the children they tracked from Grade 2 to Grade 5, those who wrote by hand as compared to those who typed on a keyboard produced more words and expressed more ideas faster and consistently. This effect was found to be comparable to that of meditation (Luders et al., 2012). As such, journaling by hand is more likely to bring you a richer and deeper experience that brings together aspects from your mind, body and soul.

In terms of what you need to get started, it is useful to consider your journaling intentions. If you are more into keeping track of work progress, meetings, fitness habits and other daily activities, a digital journal/diary could work for you. However, if you are looking to be more focused and mindful, dissect feelings or generate ideas, then writing the journal by hand is the way to go.

You could also do both—type out any information you need to record or track, and journal when you need to slow down, self-evaluate or focus.

For digital journaling, all you need could simply be Microsoft Word or any of the several cloud-based journaling applications such as Day One Journal. Hybrid journaling apps with handwriting support include GoodNotes, Evernote and Notability.

It is worth noting that acquiring the equipment for this purpose can be quite expensive, and you will have to do some extensive testing of apps to get your desired user experience. You might even be forced to pay subscription fees for attractive features and additional storage.

So what supplies do you need to get started?

EQUIPMENT FOR BEGINNERS

First, bear in mind that your equipment will not really make or break your journaling habit, but can enhance your experience.

The best equipment is simply what you love and enjoy using. This will make the experience pleasurable and help you keep up the habit. As you continue journaling, you will come to appreciate that quality is important. You will be using the items regularly, so you wouldn't want to have to deal with washed out pages or bleeding ink.

However, there is no use hoarding dozens of pens and highlighters you will probably only use once or over-the-top notebooks that cost you a little too much.

You only need a pen/pencil and a notebook to begin your very first journal. It is as simple as that. You probably have a notebook and some pens lying around somewhere in a desk drawer at work/home/school.

A good way to start is to use what you already have at your disposal before hitting the shops. It's good for the environment too. If it helps you feel more excited about the journey, you could make a little upgrade to your notebook and add a few pens. It's really up to you.

Along the way, you could be adding to your equipment one or two things at a time. The most important thing is to start journaling. And the time to start is now.

Notebooks

A notebook is the foundation of your journaling experience. It is actually the *journal.* So get one that is right for you.

Consider the very first journal you keep as a practice notebook. So do not overlook what you have already lying in the house including a composition book—which is a great starter notebook, by the way. For a few dollars, you can stock up on a couple of these, especially during the back-to-school season. They have sewn binding that secures the pages and are sturdy to carry around.

You will use your first notebook to try out your journaling style and make mistakes as you discover what is best suited for you.

How To Choose A Notebook

Use the following considerations to choose your ideal notebook, though your choice should be ultimately based on your preferences.

- **Paper quality:** This is determined by the smoothness of the paper surface and the thickness of the paper. This will also determine what pens you can write with. Smooth paper is best suited for ink pens and fountain pens. For pencils, a coarser paper may be more appropriate. A thicker paper is preferable if you prefer using gel or fountain pens to prevent bleeding and shadowing. Paper quality doesn't really matter if you are using a regular ballpoint pen.
- **Blank pages, dots, grids or lines?** It is advisable to experiment with the different styles to decide on what suits you.
- **Size:** This will mostly depend on how you intend to use it. Do you want portability, for example, or portability but with ample space to incorporate art? The sizes range from Letter (A4), Half Letter (A5), Legal (8.5 x 14), Junior Legal (8 x 5) to "pocket-size." The Half Letter and Junior Legal sizes are the most common and all-purpose sizes with the Letter-size being considered a little too big. Pocket-sized notebooks will often have much fewer pages but you can carry them with you.
- **Binding:** This is often tied to the size of the notebook; pocket-sized notebooks will often be staple bound, letter-sized ones will be spiral bound. Stitched binding is more preferred, while glue binding can be less sturdy. Spiral and glue binding tend to cause trouble in laying the notebook flat. Stitched or a combination of glue and stitched

binding is considered the best: lightweight, sturdy and the book lies flat. A stitched binding notebook will have threads on the outside spine of the book, while you'll notice a spiral bound notebook by the conspicuous metal spirals along the spine of the book.

- **Page Count:** You have to consider this in relation to the price of the notebook and come to a reasonable balance. Ideally, you want it to last a long time without limiting your expression.
- **Cover:** Again, this is based on your preference and how you journal. You can choose between a hard and soft cover. Hard covers are durable, seemingly more formal and provide a surface to write on while on the go. Others prefer a soft cover for its flexibility by allowing you to fold the notebook when needed. You can also opt for a refillable cover such as the traveler's notebook system that protects your soft-cover journals. You might choose your journal based on the picture on the front—something that feels relevant to you at the moment.
- **Price:** Probably the biggest factor here, and with a wide range of notebooks available, you should find one that fits your budget perfectly. Students can particularly benefit from discounts.

The above variables might sound intimidating as you start off, but they need not be. Just begin journaling with any notebook that you can get your hands on. Once you fill the first practice notebook and feel like you want to upgrade, you will already have a good idea of what you might like to try next time.

Pens

While there is not much mystery about pens, in journaling the pen(s) that you choose to use can significantly impact your experience. By now, you probably have a favorite pen or pencil that you either used or still use.

Having a pen that you like, is seamless to use, and/or reflects your personality can add joy to your journaling process. Make this accessory appealing to you as opposed to randomly pulling a pen out each time.

You can gradually also invest in a set of pens that feel nice to write with to help you write in your journal more often and maintain the habit.

Remember, as discussed earlier, some pens are more suited for some paper types than others. You wouldn't want to have a notebook that you can't write on with your favorite pen now, would you?

Types of Pens for Journaling

As you settle into your journaling cruise, you will realize that a pen is not just a pen. You will have a favorite pen, and you may want to have a collection of pens that keep it interesting and worth looking forward to. Choosing a pen, you will be surprised, can be a lot harder than it seems.

You have to consider factors such as the type of ink, color options and the point size. Getting these right will actually enhance the overall experience of writing in the journal. If you are inclined to experiment with pen types, below is a list to consider.

- **Ballpoint Pens:** They are the most common and well-known. They use oil-based ink that dries much faster compared to others, ensuring less smudging, and they last longer. However, they require applying more pressure when writing due to the thick ink, and as such are less ideal for long sessions of writing. Nevertheless, they are a reliable and easy option for everyday use.
- **Rollerball Pens**: Similarly designed as ballpoints, but they use water-based ink. It flows faster and unlike oil-based ink, soaks into paper more thus requiring less writing pressure. They are ideal for drafting text with fine and dark lines. Since they use water-soluble dyes, they also offer a much wider range of colors. They are better suited for writing for longer periods but you will need to up your paper thickness to be able to handle the water base.
- **Gel Pens:** By using water-based gel inks, they merge the characteristics of both the rollerball and ballpoint pen types. As such, there is less likelihood of smudging (ballpoint) and smooth writing is assured as the gel flows freely (rollerball). They also offer a wide range of colors by using pigments rather than regular dyes. It is a great choice if you are looking for both reliability and making a bold statement.
- **Marker Pens:** There are four types of inks that marker pens come in: oil, pigment, alcohol and water-based. Water and pigment-based inks are meant for writing on paper. There is a wide array of colors, types and point sizes that will accommodate both plain writing and more artistic journaling. Marker pens will be perfect for you if you are often

inclined to add a color splash to your journaling project.
- **Stylus Pens:** These are two-in-one writing tools that have a stylus on one end and a traditional pen on the other end. A stylus consists of a rubber tip that is round for use on touchscreen devices and helps keep the touchscreen free of scratches and fingerprints. You need to research the compatibility with your device and the support for handwriting if you are keeping a hybrid journal. *Capacitive* styluses are best suited for mostly navigation, while *active* styluses will give you a near-authentic pen experience for paper-like writing and drawing—they also have a useful "palm-rejection" feature that allows you to rest your palm on the screen.

Colors

With journaling being a priceless way of exploring your inner self, you can use colors to further enhance your experience.

You may normally use a black or blue pen for your everyday writing. When it comes to journaling, however, the colors you choose to use can reveal more than you are able to express verbally. That is why some people choose to keep a collection of pens, markers, crayons, paint, or coloring pencils close when they start journaling. The color you are using may help you better express yourself or learn something new about yourself.

Used consciously, colors can represent emotions (Color Therapy Blog, n.d.). For instance, blue may represent peace or sadness. Other colors include yellow (happiness), red (rage or anger), and green (envy, also hope). What's most important is the emotion that color brings out in you, what a certain color means for you.

For example, if there is one significantly sad moment in your life such as grief, and the color you associate with that is maroon, maybe because that is the color of the top you wore that day, then it might be your color for sadness or loss.

Colors can also be used to influence your mood. You might choose a color because you want to feel a certain way that day. For example, writing or drawing in yellow could give you a mood boost or red might give you some energy or courage that you need.

So if you feel colors can help you make your journaling more interesting and make you more expressive, then you should definitely give them a try.

The notebook and the pen are, in truth, all you need to start your journaling journey. Many experienced journalers believe that *the pen is mightier than the keyboard* if you are to ever get the full advantages of journaling.

In fact, that is all you might really ever need to keep your journal project going. Think of basic grooming versus accessorizing. If you are purely utilitarian, you are all about the functional or practical rather than appearing attractive or sophisticated. If you are not, you will be drawn to the decorative and elegant. For both, there is a wide range of accessories that you can add to your journaling project and make it even more fun and engaging.

Whether you are in school, college or at a point in your adult life where you realize you want more deliberate action, reflection and self-growth in your life, journaling will help you start. It will essentially *introduce you to yourself* and you can take the conversation from there.

The choice of notebook(s) and pen(s) will always be purely subjective and rightly so. With a little knowledge of what could clash, e.g., paper quality to pen type, the best use of each product and an intention to keep the project alive, you will always find something that is a fit for you. You are not under pressure to conform to what would seem to be popular styles or conventions that some would want to force onto others.

In fact, when you make the decision to start journaling, the first thing you will eventually come to evaluate is your initial ability to remain truly you and take charge of this extremely private process. You don't have to ask yourself that question now, but later on, you will look back and see the growth in your character over time—the oldest reference point being the very simple decision of starting, and the pen and notebook that you chose.

Accessories

On top of the pens/pencils and notebook(s), you could add a few additional items that could make this experience fun for you. These are by no means necessary, but depending on your personality, they could really contribute to making your journaling easier and more enjoyable.

- **Pencil/Pen bag:** A miniature pouch to contain your favorite pens and/or pencils can make moving about with your journal considerably easier. Compare this with the annoying rattling sound of pens inside

your backpack or purse. You will also be protecting your valuable pens and pencils for a longer life.
- **Ruler:** It could be the only drawing tool that you will ever use. Many prefer one that has a cork back that prevents it from slipping while in use. Clear Westcott rulers appear to be favorites for many journalers. If your portable journal has a pocket, a small ruler that fits easily could come in handy. If you would regularly be using a ruler, you should consider keeping a longer, e.g., 12-inch ruler, in the house—it is invaluable for two-page spreads.
- **A circling tool or drawing compass:** While you could avoid this expense by tracing round a bottle cap or glass, you can get a specific tool for this if circling is integral to your journaling habit. You could use a regular compass if you already have one. Alternatively, Helix has created a stencil template that has a variety of circle sizes on it. If you want to go all out, their Angle and Circle maker is a popular tool you can pick up that will help you make perfect circles of any size in your journal.
- **Post-it Notes:** You might already be in love with post-it notes. They are a familiar feature on bulletin boards, including in a private dorm room. People use them for an array of reasons including brainstorming and as reminders. In a journal, you can use them to track the progress of a particular goal, as a bookmark or to append additional information on a journal page if you run out of space. Post-it notes are incredibly useful and popular with journal keepers.
- **Stickers:** There are thousands of stickers available from across the world to add some gorgeous design, charm or art into your journaling project. While

this could be seen as purely aesthetic, it can help you make your experience fun, worth looking forward to and feel like less of a chore. Even the stickers you choose to embellish your journal pages can over time become a record of how your tastes and preferences are changing. The imagery created can also connect you to your writing at a deeper level.

- **Washi tape:** Essentially a Japanese paper masking tape that is decorative, thin and durable, coming in hundreds of patterns and colors. Why would it be an accessory for your journaling? If you are the artistic type, the Washi tape enables you to effortlessly (within seconds) add colorful design and flair to your journal. And there is something for everyone from hundreds of sizes, patterns, textures and colors. Enthusiasts caution that if you catch the Washi tape bug, you could end up with a collection of ridiculous proportions.

- **Paper adhesive:** It offers a quick way to add things (printables or pictures) to your journal. This may be because you do not want to draw, you want to save time or you are very sure that particular thing belongs on that particular page. You can add basically anything you desire, including doodles, quotes and pictures. Permanent adhesive tapes are much better than glue since you will avoid chances of wrinkling pages or a spill. They can also be nifty enough to fit inside your pencil pouch.

- **White-out:** Expect that you will make mistakes and decide how you would want to handle them. For some of us, journals should be mistake-free zones or in the least, they should be a tad neater than our regular writing. If that is you, then whiteout will be your friend. Consider dry white-out tape for its marginal invisibility and no time to dry. If you are at home with not covering your mistakes, a strikethrough will work just fine. The writing mistakes you make could fairly be deemed as part of your journey.

- **Watercolors:** If you are planning on being a little artsy with your reflection and planning, there are several watercolor sets to choose from. They include brands such as Prang which is inexpensive, Dr. Ph. Martin's hydrus liquid watercolors (concentrated), Sennelier (velvety) and Coliro (metallic).
- **Paint brushes:** These will go hand in hand with your watercolors. You want them to be durable, dependable and comfortable to use without much fuss. These two accessories are very niche if you are not trying to be artsy with your journal. For others, they could be essential. Try out the Grumbacher and Pentel brands if you are unsure.

The above shortlist is just the tip of the iceberg when it comes to the many accessories that you can acquire to make your journaling experience fun and tailored for you. You can consider them in the future after starting your journey in the simplest way possible.

I would not be surprised if in a years' time you have amassed all manner of stationery once you have committed to this rewarding habit!

The entire journaling community could be said to have a sort of obsession with stationery, but everyone has their own sweet spot. The biggest mistake you can do is attempt to match up to another's would-be *standards*. You will be taking away from the privacy and individuality of the journaling process.

As you grow into the habit, you could be creating a wish list of supplies you would want to add to your journaling project and let your equipment grow organically. If you are to not lose sight of the main objective of journaling, you should really start small and concentrate on putting your thoughts, ideas, feelings, aspirations and so forth on paper. You still have all the time in the world to shop for the fancy accessories that your heart desires once you are on track.

The most important thing that you need to do is start now with what you have.

3

WHAT DO I NEED? A PLACE WHERE I CAN JOURNAL

KEEPING YOUR JOURNAL SAFE

One thing that you need to really hold dear from this book is how private and individual journaling is. Perhaps some of the most accessible parallels we can draw would be the login details to your social media profiles.

It is inconceivable that you would share them even with your closest friend or family. Your online identity is probably more guarded than your actual lived experience, which is a little surprising, but with good reason given the largely superficial world we now live in.

If you are really intentional about journaling and reaping the full benefits, then you would be seriously inclined to protect your journal's contents.

Sure, it is true that some of us will make their journals accessible to their partners or other trusted confidantes. Some journal keepers have actually expressed their dilemma between keeping their journals fully private and the guilt of keeping *secrets* from their loved ones.

In my experience, most people would be more comfortable keeping their journals strictly confidential, sometimes under lock and key depending on the environment they are living in. This is with good reason. If there is a high chance that *unauthorized* people will be perusing through your journal—basically taking an unguided tour through your brain's private vault—and you cannot protect against this, you will be less likely to be honest in the journal. Being honest with yourself is essential and the doorway to all of the benefits of journaling.

GETTING COMFORTABLE WITH THE UNCOMFORTABLE

Effective journaling is intricately intertwined with vulnerability. Now, I know vulnerability is not an everyday concept, so let's try to understand it. Unlike keeping a diary, as we have discussed before, journaling is more engaging, self-reflective and forward-looking than merely documenting activities and tracking tasks to stay organized.

A typical dictionary definition of vulnerability is *the state or quality of being exposed to the possibility of being harmed or attacked, either emotionally or physically.* So it is a state where you are unable to control the effects of the environment around you. During an episode of vulnerability, your protection or defense is either lacking, diminished, ineffective or compromised. You are, in a sense, at the mercy of the environment.

But in journaling, you are not really helpless as the formal definition of vulnerability would imply. You are consciously letting your guard down. Why? To fully engage with your feelings, emotions, insecurities, aspirations, half-formed ideas, and so on, without the hindrances that characterize the public persona you portray. You deliberately take a step out of your comfort zone and pour out your heart and soul on paper.

Vulnerability in this sense is like being naked, but by yourself. No one is judging you and you are not trying to lie to yourself. This is the precise environment that reflective journaling will be most potent if you are to add richness to your life. You are also not aiming to beat yourself up, while you are vulnerable. It is important that you are gentle with yourself while you are intentionally being vulnerable.

Hopefully it is now clear why those who keep journals would go to a large extent to keep them very private. Related to this, how possible is it to have privacy when journaling? The first step is to consider your environment.

It is important that you are comfortable with the space where you are going to be journaling. That if you are not at ease, then you are likely not to be as honest when recording your daily thoughts, feelings, experiences and goals. You may also find it hard to concentrate and settle into the activity. This could be compared to the feeling you have that keeps you looking behind you while walking along a dark street at night.

CREATING A JOURNALING SANCTUARY

Full-time writers would be most familiar with the importance of creating a writing sanctuary. They could tell you about the incredible impact on the quality of work they are able to produce. You could also call it solitude, but far from the negative connotation, it is that dedicated space where many beloved authors have been able to get into their element and produce priceless works.

Famous British author and screenwriter Roald Dahl is fondly remembered not just for literary treasures such as *Charlie and the Chocolate Factory*, but also for reinforcing the potency of solitude in creative writing.

The former wartime pilot transformed a shed inside his garden into a writing sanctuary—an intensely personal space that assured him full concentration. The hut has since been turned into a museum. Here is what he said about his writing sanctuary:

> *"When I am up here I see only the paper I am writing on, and my mind is far away with Willy Wonka or James or Mr. Fox or Danny or whatever else I am trying to cook up. The room itself is of no consequence. It is out of focus, a place for dreaming and floating and whistling in the wind, as soft and silent and murky as a womb."*
>
> — ROALD DAHL (WHITE, 2017)

We are probably not as privileged to have a garden shed that we can convert into a writing space as Dahl, whose books sold over 250 million copies across the world. Journaling is also not full-time writing, nor are we intending to publish our thoughts for anyone who cares to read. However, the concept of a writing haven still applies to our very private writing.

The journaling sanctuary doesn't have to be complicated or

elaborate as long as it serves the purpose as succinctly put by Dahl above. You can create your ideal writing space literally anywhere.

Your perfect journaling space can be anywhere from the kitchen table, to a spare room, to a corner of the living room. It's up to you, really. So, do not overthink it. The idea is to have a space with an element of solitude that you can come back to regularly, and where you can write your journal with minimal to no distractions. That said, it doesn't have to be static either. Since circumstances change, it is even more important to know how that personal space makes you feel so that you are able to recreate it somewhere else if and when you need to.

It must be suitably chosen such that when you are there, you are encouraged to be vulnerable with yourself and express your thoughts and reflections in an unrestrained manner. Remember, journaling is not supposed to take too much of your time, so it should be fairly easy to find a quiet spot for a 20-minute-or-so journaling session.

YOUR UNIQUE SPACE

We have included an overview of the types of things that you might want to consider when creating your own unique journaling sanctuary. As well as the practical considerations above, here is some advice about how to set up the environment itself and ways you can experiment with how you use your space:

- **Make it comfy:** The desk and chair (traditionally) will be the very place where all the action happens. It is important to make sure that it is comfortable. Full-time writers go to great lengths to set up what would essentially be called a workspace, making it as comfortable as possible. But for journaling, getting comfy does not in any way mean getting new furniture. It could be your favorite couch, the kitchen table, or the chill-out space on the terrace. You might simply want to prop yourself up and sit on the edge of a cushion on the floor. Basically, whatever works for you.

If your space involves a desk and chair, you might want to consider adjustable lower back support, a standing desk or bar-height stool and table. You might also want to consider extra cushioning on the chair, floor, or bed if it makes you more comfortable.

- **Clutter:** There is no consensus in the journaling community on whether what would be considered clutter should be eliminated from the space, or if it could actually be helpful. Everyone has their own preference, and you can design your space to give you maximum concentration and inspiration. Some studies show that working in a neat, clutter-free environment is associated with generally healthier habits while other studies show that those who work in messy environments or what could be termed *organized chaos* tend to be more creative and uninhibited.
- **Keep sources of inspiration close:** Some people find it useful to have inspiration nearby. The point is not having just physical articles that you can draw inspiration from. It can also be virtual, such as from Pinterest. Visual reminders are useful for many people. They can help you flesh out your abstract ideas as well as providing motivation to get started.

You can add any meaningful objects to your wall, shelf, desktop, bulletin board, or even the notebook itself. It could also be simply a quote or picture on the wall in front of you that is very important to you.
- **Keep your tools within reach:** We are busy, and unlike full-time writers, journaling is a self-evaluation tool and not a career. We will almost always have no more than about half an hour to jot down our thoughts and ideas. It is essential that the equipment you need is all within reach when you settle down to journal.

From pens to notebooks to markers and other fun accessories, they all have to be where you need them to be. This is where your pen/pencil bag can be invaluable if you want to stay organized and save time. You do not want your flow of thoughts to be interrupted just because you needed to go to another room to find a pen in a different color or a highlighter for some important idea that just came to you.

- **Keep distractions at bay:** Some people would be perfectly fine journaling every day after lunch at a coffee shop regardless of the occupancy. Others are more likely to be distracted by noise, making the entire journaling experience a nightmare. If this is you, closing windows, doors and any source of unwelcome sound, including music, could work for you as you can block out the world. Alternatively, you could be the kind of person that can barely write if there is no noise. In this case, you might want to keep your windows open or play some music.

There is also the issue of digital disruption from gadgets such as your smartphone, laptop and chiefly, social media. For these, you have options such as turning your phone off, putting it on silent mode or scheduling your email and notification checks so that they do not overlap with your journaling time. Even more important, you have to determine the level of control you have on the environment around your journaling sanctuary. Will your housemates blast music while you are journaling? Can you keep the fan on or windows open without disturbing your mates? These are all things to take into consideration.

- **Take advantage of your senses:** When we talk about creating an environment where your journaling can thrive, it is really all about your senses. You want them to be engaged, and encouraging you into the mood for journaling when you are in your sanctuary. Many journal keepers prefer candles with a cozy warm glow, some incense or an aromatherapy diffuser. What aromas do you enjoy? Another aspect of this, is if you are consistent with the scent and supplies you use, you will be tuning your brain every time it gets these stimuli to know that it is "journaling time."

Based on your experience, a different scent once in a while could help you achieve a targeted mood for a specific idea, feeling or problem you want to dissect. Music and soundtracks can also enable you to create an ambiance that can help you get focused. There are dozens of other ways to enliven your senses including brewing some tea (taste) and the texture of the objects around you (touch).

- **Make it an emotional and physical space:** As I

pointed out earlier, journaling and privacy go hand in hand. A good way to decide on the spaces that will work as journaling havens is to look at what emotional and physical factors could come in the way of you keeping up with this habit. Even if your family or roommates generally respect your privacy, you have to get more assurance that you are safe to be vulnerable with yourself.

Even the mere fact that you are too familiar with a certain space could be a physical distraction. Colleagues, family and friends, as well as associated memories in a certain space, could emotionally prevent you from being in your element. As you start journaling, you might find it useful to think about how various spaces, people or scenarios affect your ability to fully go inward into your reflective space.

- **Create a ritual:** One of the popular ways to create a sanctuary for your journaling is thinking about it in terms of rituals. Now, I know not everyone has consistent daily rituals, so this might not be for you. However, this does not mean you cannot make journaling your first-ever ritual.

Even for those without strict rituals, there are some things that are constant, such as making breakfast, brushing your teeth or even praying before bed. It would be easy to choose a point in any of these repeated daily actions to practice your journaling. For instance, you could write your journal on the kitchen table while your morning coffee brews, or on the bedside table just before you turn your lights off to go to sleep. You can also steal a few minutes of your working day or lunch break at school to sit in the car, windows rolled down, or by the canal enjoying the fresh air as you journal.

The point is to make it part of your routine. If you are journaling every day, you want it to be as close to your daily schedule as possible. You will be glad to know that we explore this topic in more detail in Chapter 5 after you have tried your first writing.

As I have said throughout this book, there are no dos and don'ts in journaling. Any journal keeper you meet will have their own unique story about their journaling spaces. Even when you think you have created a space that you could actually call a sanctuary, do not make the mistake of shackling yourself to that space.

Over time your journaling goals and needs will evolve, and the space may not necessarily fit your new needs. It could even get just plain boring, causing you to lose your inspiration. Therefore, you do not have to write in that space every single time if you do not feel like it.

The journal sanctuary can also evolve to become a mental space rather than necessarily having to be a physical space, allowing you to switch locations and still achieve the same level of concentration that you require. It is also perfectly okay to want to keep and cherish a dedicated physical place where you feel at home connecting with your thoughts. The key is to figure out what, and not necessarily where, gets you in the right headspace for journaling.

You may find that you collect a number of spaces where your journaling is easy and remains private. You may use different spaces for different focuses, such as a room with a view for inspiration and creativity and a comfy space for more of a hideaway sanctuary that is relaxing where you can write about more difficult material.

Your spaces could vary from true solitude, where you are

completely by yourself, to other places where you are more connected to the outside world such as staying in a coffee shop after lunch to write for 20 minutes. You have access to a number of different levels of connection/solitude and you can choose your level on that day. The highest level of solitude would be when you are completely isolated from the familiar, for example taking a trip to have a whole night at a hotel away from home. This level of distance from your day-to-day life can be very useful when you are trying to get some perspective.

All in all, the unique personal spaces you construct for yourself should have everything you need to inspire you to be honest and vulnerable with yourself and offer you a brief shelter from the ups and downs of life. They will also, over time, hopefully bring you a level of joy and satisfaction that makes you want to go there again and again.

4

WHERE DO I START? START HERE

> *"After I had come home from work last Thursday, I sat in the car outside the house for 20 minutes in silence. When I managed to go inside, I could barely speak to my wife. It was all I could do to go straight to bed."*
>
> — COLLINS, 2018

The above is an entry from the journal of Bryan Collins—a nonfiction author and Forbes columnist. At a time when he was contemplating a defining career move, he reviewed his old journal posts and found the above which, among others, helped him make the decision to leave his current job.

Forget about the big decision that was made and the many other factors that could have helped him make up his mind and focus on how natural that journal entry was. It spoke the honest truth of how his life was being affected and brought out what was important at a critical moment.

It wasn't written on the day that the final decision was made. It was also quite brief but descriptive enough to give a good snapshot of that defining moment. He was able to use it as an aid to make a big decision months later.

WRITE DOWN YOUR "WHY"

It is one thing to think about starting journaling, and a completely different thing to actually start doing it. Understanding that is a real game changer.

A year or even five could easily pass by with the plan to start a journal still very real in your mind, probably as some of our New Year's resolutions turn out to be—unrealized intentions.

You may have the notion, as many do, that to keep a journal, you have to sit and write a lot in poetic language on your ideas. But it's really all about finding a quiet time and thinking about yourself. You could simply write about what you did or felt that day such as from the Bryan Collins example, or putting in words something that you just couldn't get off your mind, or a conversation that inspired you.

Sometimes you could have so much to write about that it goes into a couple of pages. Other times, it might be just a few lines. Think of it only as a commitment to slow down a little and take a moment to think about the things going on in your life. No one else is going to be reading your journal, so personalize it as much as you can.

A good way to get started is to stop and think about the reason you want to start a journal. Your first journal entry could actually be an answer to two questions. *Why do I want to start keeping a journal? What do I hope to get out of this?*

Write down the answers to these questions in your journal.

The answers to these two questions will help you maintain your journaling habit by constantly reminding you of the "why" that you have defined for yourself. They will also help you start to find the most suitable journaling style for you. We learn best by doing, so the rest of your answers will come later after you have tried out journaling for a little while. Don't expect to know your "style" from Day 1.

Copying out your why (or a summary of your why) in the front cover of your journal can be useful inspiration each time you open your book. It can also act like an important reminder in the same way as pinning a post at the top of a Facebook group does.

START ANYWHERE

Just as with the choice of equipment, you do not need to start with anything that you do not already have. You can start with what is on your mind right now. This could be assignments that are forthcoming if you are a student, work deadlines, new ideas, thoughts about your friendship circle, relationships, family life, and so on.

By writing about what is right on top of your mind when you decide to journal, you will be surprised at how many thoughts and reflections that you will be able to come up with right away.

An easy way to start journaling is to write about your day. Who you met, what you did, something you said, what you learned, and so on. Did you see something that really "wowed" you today? Were you bored and drifted off? Did you go to a party and have too much to drink? Had an argument with a friend? The more you write, the easier it will get, but don't feel under pressure to write a lot on Day 1. See what comes naturally. If you are struggling, it can help to start with simply writing, "I am not sure what to write in my journal today," and then the next thing that pops into your head.

TYPES OF JOURNALS

Like I mentioned earlier, there isn't a lot of structure when it comes to journaling. Every person is free to personalize and customize it in their own way, which means that there are several types of journals.

Below are some of the common types of journals that are popular among journalers. You can pick one from this list that works for you, or create your own unique type of journal if none of these works for you.

- **Bullet Journal:** This is one of the popular journal types for goal setting and productivity. It uses either a dot grid or blank notebook where you create sections for, among others, daily to-dos, weekly or monthly calendars, making notes, tracking your activities, recording short and long-term goals, and so on. It's called a bullet journal because of the use of shorthand or "rapid logging," where instead of full sentences, you shorten entries into keywords or short phrases. Since there is no predetermined template, you use the dot grid or blank page to create something that fits your needs.
- **Dream Journal:** This is a journal dedicated to your dreams. They could be the actual dreams you have while asleep, or the dreams you have about your life. After waking up, you write about the dream(s) you had or the things you plan for yourself in the future.

- **The Guided Journal:** This is a great choice for anyone who is starting and is not used to writing a lot. With a guided journal, you are less likely to stare at a page wondering what to write. It contains writing prompts which could be questions to answer or a topic. You can write, paint, draw or add photos, and so on in response to the prompts. You can choose one based on your goals, including self-explorations, habit-formation, happiness, goal-setting, and so on. They contain a range of prompts, including very simple ones and very provocative ones.
- **The Gratitude Journal:** Want to focus on the positive things in your life? The gratitude journal is designed to enable you record the things you are grateful for, however small, as you start and finish the day. People who have kept gratitude journals say it helps them focus on *what really matters*, among other benefits.
- **Mental Health Journal:** If your focus is your mental well-being, you can keep this kind of a journal and log your feelings—the good, the bad and the ugly. Note, however, that this is not a substitute for professional therapy. If you would like some more structured support, there is a list of organizations at the end of this book.
- **The Artist's Journal:** If you are artsy, you can keep a visual record of your ideas and thoughts. Typically, visuals such as doodles and drawings are combined with words. The journal can also have text-only entries.
- **The Brainstorm Journal:** You use this to record any good ideas that come to you in the course of the day before they are forgotten. For this kind of journal, it

is advisable to always have your journal with you on the go. Potentially something small stored in a pocket.
- **Morning Pages:** First thing every morning, open your journal and write about two pages in longhand of whatever comes to mind. Allow your stream of consciousness to flow into paper without really *thinking*.
- **Classic "Dear Diary" Journal:** With this kind of journal, you write without any guidelines. You could write a few paragraphs today, 3 pages tomorrow, and so on. You make it whatever it needs to be for you—to celebrate, ponder, grieve, organize and process your feelings.

There are several other journal types based on various topics and needs, including food/diet, pregnancy, fitness, travel, family, projects and so on. Do you know what you want to use your journal for?

START NOW

Follow these steps to start journaling today:

1. Set aside time: You may not have any time limits, but if you do, you could set a timer for 10 minutes or however long you have got. This will help you focus on your journaling and not worry about keeping an eye on the time.

- If you still have more to write after the time is up, ask yourself whether you have time to keep going and set the timer again.
- Even on a busy day, you can schedule a brief timed session to journal.

2. Make your first entry: This is the most important step in your journaling project. Decide on the kind of journal you want to try out, and start writing what is on your mind.

- If you are not sure, try logging what happened during the day, who you talked to, how you felt, what you did or didn't accomplish, your joys and frustrations.
- Like I said above, you could start with the sentence "I am not sure what to write in my journal today" and then the next thing that pops into your head.
- You could add a drawing or doodle if you feel like it.

3. Add a date: It can be useful to track the day, or even the time of day you wrote something. A full date at the top is recommended if you are writing regularly or, alternatively, you might want to use other cues that will remind you of that particular moment when you come back to read.

4. Let the writing flow: Do not be too critical of yourself or doubt what you are writing down. You do not need to make corrections as you write. This is your story, your truth at this moment. So embrace the beauty of writing for yourself and express your deepest thoughts.

- It can help to picture yourself speaking to someone, a friend maybe and write down what you would say. The process of writing down your thoughts can help to fully grasp them.
- Explore any feelings or emotions that come up. Try to write about why you feel that way.

5. Take a moment to reflect: Sometimes, you might find it hard to get the flow. Take a moment to slow down before you start writing. Listen to what you are feeling.

COMMON BLOCKS TO STARTING

You do have the intention to start journaling, but you may be discouraged from beginning by a number of factors. Keeping a journal requires some mental and physical presence to achieve your desired results, you might not think you are truly capable of writing a journal, or you might view it as a task or chore. Some level of motivation is needed to start writing, which is something even professional writers face every day.

Some of the common blocks to starting include:

Writer's Block

This is the feeling of being stuck on what to write. You feel like your mind is blank and there is nothing in it to write about. Alternatively, it might be that there are many competing ideas that are clogging your mind. This is making it hard for you to pick one.

What to do: If you experience writer's block, you might find it useful to begin with a guided journal. The prompts in a guided journal will give you a specific topic to write about so you don't have to pick one. Another way to make it easier for you to make meaningful entries about your day is to keep some journaling prompts that you like at hand in the beginning.

On the other hand, if you are paralyzed by competing thoughts, you could write them down in a list or in thought bubbles until they are all written out. Then you can pick one to start exploring in more detail. There is more help for this type of situation in Chapter 8, which you can read as a standalone chapter and then come back to this if you like, right now.

Difficulty Getting The Perfect Words

If you view journaling as a task you must complete, you could have many false starts trying to achieve some level of perfection with your language.

What to do: Try to bear in mind that no one is really grading your entries, and you are the only intended audience. So instead of worrying about writing flawlessly, focus on letting your thoughts flow onto paper, and you can correct later if you need to. You can use shorthand, drawings, pictures or other non-text entries if that is what works best for you. Remind yourself that you are writing for your eyes only. Instead of being your worst critic, be your best supporter. Own it; it's your voice.

Write about whatever you want, using the tools that you like and at a time and place that suits you. This will help you to both keep your thoughts flowing and build confidence.

Must It Be A Paper Journal?

You will more often than not be advised to keep a pen-and-paper journal due to the therapeutic benefits of writing by hand. But what if this does not work for you? You will be glad to know that some journal keepers will keep both a paper journal and a digital journal or exclusively journal on their laptops.

If you find it inconvenient to keep a paper journal, you can always go with the keyboard. Do not allow this to prevent you from starting your journaling. Some journalers argue that they find writing with the keyboard more productive and that it allows their consciousness to stream through more easily, in fact. They also say they find it faster and thus convenient for their busy lives.

What to do: Try a few things out and ask yourself which feels right. Experiment with a paper journal, your laptop or smartphone and see how journaling in those ways makes you feel. Are you going to obsess over your handwriting rather than the ideas and thoughts, or does the screen potentially introduce new distractions to you? If words are the issue, could an art journal be the best starting point for you? Daily doodles and sketches with minimal words could be your thing.

Here are some additional tips to deal with common blocks to starting journaling:

- You don't have to journal first thing in the morning if this puts you off and all you can think about is your first cup of coffee. It can be at any point in the day.
- Start small and set realistic expectations.
- Your journal is personal, it's okay to be messy.
- Explore all the formats, and go with whatever format you feel like at a particular time.
- If you want to build it into your regular routine, make a decision about when and where you will journal and how often. We will talk about this more in the next chapter.

Remember, since journaling is a personal pursuit, you can't get it wrong.

CARVING OUT SPACE IN YOUR DAY

One of the common reasons people give for never keeping up the habit of journaling is *not having the time.* This is true for many beginners who start off with grand expectations. But if you start out small for the next couple of days and weeks, you can create the space for it and turn it into a habit.

It does not matter how many words you end up writing. Try this example and see how easy it is to create time within your regular day to jot something down.

For just one minute a day, say when waiting for your coffee to heat up in the microwave, during an ad break on the TV or in between lectures, grab a piece of paper and pick just one thing to try and write about:

- one thing you are thankful for,
- one thing you think you'd want to brag about,
- one thing that is worrying you, or
- one thing you desire.

That's it! Try doing this for a week and see how it makes you feel about recording your thoughts and the ability to create space for journaling. Chances are it could very well lead to something bigger.

CARVING OUT SPACE FOR JOURNALING

In Chapter 3, we talked about the idea of creating a personal space or "sanctuary" for journaling that enables you to get into the journaling headspace with little to no distraction. We emphasized the need for privacy so that you can be truly "you" during that brief moment of self-reflection.

The sanctuary need not be static, depending on your daily schedule, whether you are in school, work or home. If you are often on the move, you may have to look for temporary sanctuary in a place you think will give you the best chance at concentration with the most privacy.

Carving out space to journal, the goal of this section, is more about helping you allocate time within your regular schedule to put your thoughts, feelings, goals and so on down regularly. Your life was already busy or perhaps well-defined before venturing into this project, which means you might feel like you have to squeeze journaling into what you already have.

The only way you will make it work is by carving out the space first and then putting journaling into that space. So, think about what you can do less of in your week or what activity you are going to take those daily minutes from—in order to give them to your new journaling habit.

You are new to journaling and it will take some work, intentional work for that matter, to make it into a habit.

CHOOSE WHEN AND FOR HOW LONG TO JOURNAL

Make a definite decision about when you are going to try journaling in your day or week. Include your new habit in your daily planning so you have a reminder set. This might be on your to-do list or you set a reminder on your phone—however you usually plan. This will make it much more likely that you remember to do it and find the time to fit it in.

How often do you want to journal to start with (you can always change this later)? Make this decision now so that you can plan your journaling sessions into your week. You might like the idea of building this into every day or perhaps something like 3 times a week when you know you have some quieter moments in your schedule.

In addition to journaling at a specific time of the day or week, ensure that you have some predetermined duration that you want to spend journaling. Of course, this can be amended whenever you want to and you can have exceptions. But, in general, if you have given yourself a maximum of half an hour, try to stick to that unless you have good reason to overrun.

Giving yourself longer than you need to journal could have disadvantages such as overthinking and the pressure to perfect the writing. At the other end of the spectrum, you might not want to automatically cut short your free flow of thoughts if today they are overflowing and you feel you want to keep going. You will get to understand what works for you through experimenting with different lengths of time and rules you set for yourself.

KEEP THE GOAL SMALL

A choice of time also stops you from feeling that your new journaling habit is time consuming. You are at liberty to assign any amount of time that you deem appropriate from your normal schedule, including just 5 minutes.

As you start, keep your goals small and you will be giving yourself a chance to be more consistent. Small goals also means you are less likely to view journaling as a chore, which will improve your chances of making it a habit that you look forward to.

TOO BUSY TO JOURNAL?

Yeah, I get it. We already have a life going on and probably can barely even keep up with what is required of us. Won't journaling be an additional burden? The answer is No.

One simple hack that can help you wrestle away this feeling of being too occupied to take a small break is to just write one line per day. It is simple, non-time-consuming and a practical start to your journaling life. You can write just one single line every morning, evening or whenever else you can, however busy you are. A quick note that could turn into a big idea.

If you are looking into developing an idea or product, you should not underestimate the potential of keeping a record of your daily thoughts on it. Your brain has the ability to turn these daily one-line prompts into full-blown solutions given some time to work on it in the background while you get on with your day to day. Consider keeping your journal as close to you as possible such that you can record your most brilliant ideas before the excitement wears off and you forget all about them.

If you get into this way of journaling, you can get a journal created just for this purpose—The **One-line-a-day journal: A Five-Year Memory Book**. This is a guided journal you can purchase that literally enables you to keep five years' worth of memories in a single book, one line a day.

One unique feature of this journal is that you can see a particular day's entries for each of the five years on one page, e.g., January 1, 2021, January 1, 2022, and so on.

UTILIZE "KILLING TIME" FOR JOURNALING

Every now and then, you will have moments where you have a lot of *time to kill*—often, these are situations beyond your control such as being stuck in traffic, a delayed flight or work/school break.

This is one of the best times to journal, instead of scrolling through your phone. You will actually be much more productive and save time. This is more doable if you carry your journal with you or have a pocket-size journal for travels.

If you work or study from home, keep it near your work area and utilize the time you are waiting for meetings to get started to make some notes. Using a few minutes of your transition time after you wake up or before you sleep could also be a non-taxing way to fit some journaling in.

COLLECT FUN JOURNAL PROMPTS

For those of you that want even more structure, this can help.

Put together a collection of interesting journaling prompts that you would find exciting to think and write about. Examples of prompts include: What's something you are really good at? Where were you 10 years ago? What holds you back?

You will find a rich repository of journaling prompts on the internet to get you started. All you need to do is search for "journaling prompts" and collect as many favorites as you need to get started. You might want to refresh this every few weeks or months.

Keep them in a text, word document or write them down on the first page(s) of your notebook and journal through the list one at a time. You could even write each on a piece of paper, fold and keep them in an ideas jar and pick one at random for each day.

Each day you can journal on a different prompt. You are effectively allocating one prompt to each session that you book with yourself. You have then chosen both the time and the topic for each session.

If you keep a list of prompts like this, then when the time comes to sit down and journal, you reduce your chances of having to stare blankly at the page. Some people also find it useful to have some journal prompts as backup inspiration for blank days where they are normally writing about whatever is at the forefront of their minds.

START WITH LISTS

Another simple way to get started without finding journaling too engrossing to create enough time for is making it about lists.

List inspiring quotes, books you would want to read or have

read, your goals, favorite recipes, dreams and even daydreams. Are you considering making a major decision such as the major you should choose, whether you should leave your partner, whether you should go for that job or where to spend this year's vacation?

It could be both fun and helpful to list all the options you have about a particular choice you have to make and leave them there or come back later to cross out the least appealing alternatives. There is no pressure at all to write full sentences or paragraphs. This is just a snapshot of a moment in your life and if your record makes sense to you, then why not?

With lists, you can also use your journal as a planner—things you need to do for the week, what you have accomplished, and so on.

In summary, you are more likely to keep up the journaling habit if you intentionally carve out space to do so within your day or week. To be encouraged to do so, you have to be clear about the very reason why you want to start journaling.

As I mentioned earlier, it helps to make your first journal entry about why you wanted to keep a journal in the first place. If you have not done this yet—do it now. You can then refer back to these reasons whenever you feel unsure about where you are heading. Where, how often and what to journal about is all entirely up to you—there are no rules! So make it as easy and fun as possible for yourself when you are starting out.

FIRST STEPS IN WRITING TO YOURSELF

"Better to write for yourself and have no public, than to write for the public and have no self."

— CYRIL CONNOLLY [THE NEW STATESMAN, FEBRUARY 25, 1933]

We kick off this chapter with one of the most contested pieces of advice in writing. Should you write for yourself or for an audience?

Connolly was a British writer and literary critic who, besides authoring several influential books, was the editor of *Horizon*, a revered literary magazine. He famously advised writers to write for themselves rather than their audience, to be vulnerable with their readers if they were to get the best out of themselves.

Those who support the idea of writing for yourself say it frees you from the need to impress or the temptation to entertain, and therefore gives you the freedom to put down what you need to. You allow yourself to be transparent and honest with your writing and get the chance to articulate a message that is unique.

SELF-EXAMINATION

Greek philosopher Socrates is remembered for, among many other things, having talked about the mistake of living an unexamined life. The most literal interpretations have been about distinguishing the human from an animal—that just working, eating and procreation doesn't make a human any different from say, a zebra. What makes humans different is the ability to think and reflect upon their actions—giving love, joy and generosity at the right time and place, and believing, bettering and learning (Plato in twelve volumes, 1914).

Writing for yourself is one of the most powerful tools that you have at your disposal for self-examination. Unlike writing for profit, when the only audience is *you*, you can call yourself out and work toward solving your own problem(s), without worrying about others' reaction to your writing.

Writing for yourself gives you the freedom to switch off the internal critic in you, allowing you to be more sincere. Then your passion is unlocked—your own worldview, that has a chance of attracting more people than it would if it appeared like a copy of everyone else or fake.

Professional writers will have a great deal of time to correctly position their content to the audiences they are targeting. But in journaling, we are not writing to earn a profit or for an audience. Even as starters, our objective is to add richness to our lives, to understand ourselves better, make better decisions, give us a better shot at achieving our goals, and so on.

To kickstart your self-examination through journaling, you could ask yourself one of the following questions:

- What did I enjoy today?
- What worked well today?
- What did I find frustrating?
- What upset me? Or is bugging me right now?
- What things tend to get me really angry?
- What do I prioritize in my day? In my life?
- What unhealthy or unproductive habits might I have? What do I want to change?

As you try to answer these questions in your journal, do not just think about the *what*. Instead, you want to go the distance and figure out the *why* as well. From there, the next step is to start coming up with possible solutions. Try writing in full rant-mode and see what it does for you. Follow where it leads you and try to process it. You may be tempted to be too modest or to try and make excuses for yourself. However, if you do so, you will be ruining the whole self-discovery journey. You want to put everything on record in all honesty.

SO WHERE DO I BEGIN?

Now that we have understood why writing for yourself is so powerful, how do you begin to do so and not feel confused?

Write About Your Day

This is plainly the simplest way to keep a journal. In fact when most people think about journaling, chances are they are thinking about keeping a log of what happened every day. It is a very straightforward way of journaling—you just write down anything from that day that is important for you.

Now, a note on the word *important*. What if nothing *important* happened today? That is when we go back to our first questions—Why do I want to start keeping a journal? What do I hope to get out of this? That framework will help you to decide what qualifies as *relevant* to go into your journal from each day. Indeed, it is understandable that you may not have exhaustively answered these questions yet and still need more time to fully decide what should go into your journal. But this might help focus your mind so you can find what you want to *start* writing about. If not, the simple answer to this is *just write anything*, literally. Anything from that day.

You will be amazed by the sheer volume of things that happen in a single day. Lectures, conversations, walks, commutes, bills and purchases, questions, dilemmas, emergencies, news (media), worries, affirmations, decisions, surprises, memories . . . I could go on. There is so much happening to us, around and within us that we can write about.

Let us begin with the morning (or for night owls, whenever your typical day begins). Do you have a morning routine that is consistent? Well, even then, there are bound to be some differences. Many people prefer journaling the moment they wake up or during breakfast. You could talk about yesterday or last night if you haven't already journaled about it, or you could add anything you hadn't thought of then.

You could also write about how your morning feels, what you are looking forward to, what your goals for the day are, a quote or anything else (maybe including a list) that inspires you that morning, what you thought of in the shower, the tasks for the day and so on.

In the evening, you have many options. Choose from every single thing that happened during the day: "I woke up early/late," "My pet/housemate/partner/neighbor did this and that," "My breakfast was like this, maybe I should try this and that recipe" . . . "I actually think I should be taking homemade food to work/school instead of buying lunch," or "I am thankful I don't have to cook—I already have it paid up with my hostel and school canteen." "Mom/dad/bro/sis called to say hi . . . it's been a while," "Caleb surprised me with some cupcakes," "My favorite TV show was cancelled," "Visited the railroad museum over lunch break—oh my, it took me forever to do so!"

You can also journal about what you intend to do the following day, such as, "Must meet my boss tomorrow on my choice of candidates for the new role," "It's my cousin's birthday tomorrow, I can't make it, but I must call before 10am," and so forth.

If you have a portable journal, you could choose to write about your day *as it happens* instead; between classes, during lunch, on the metro, coffee break or whenever time allows. You are able to blend it with your day-to-day activities without feeling burdened. Need to quickly write down something urgent you must do tomorrow? Did you just schedule a meeting with a job prospect? Heard a truly inspiring quote? An idea for a blog post, dissertation topic or company presentation just hit you? Your pocket/portable journal has got you.

Record And Process Your Feelings, Opinions and Emotions

We are sensual beings. We touch and feel, we make eye contact, we perceive smell, and sound. We also judge, know when and how we are being judged (not always), hold opinions, express them and either accept (passively or actively) or reject others' opinions, express or suppress our feelings but nevertheless feel them somewhere, and as social beings, experience a range of emotions as we interact with everybody else.

The above (and so much more) causes us to have an inexhaustible goldmine of journaling material that we can choose to record and reflect on. For example, "I felt a little intimidated during today's staff meeting," "Jane's advice last night really helped me handle that difficult conversation with my partner. I think I owe her," "I don't think the product launch plan that was proposed is the best idea. I have two more days to figure out before the final meeting," "I think there is something worrying dad, I should have lunch with him tomorrow," "I feel quite confused about today's lecture. I must book a meeting with the professor."

But do not just stop at recording what you felt. Instead, try to process it as well. For example, why did you feel intimidated during the staff meeting? Is it because you were not well prepared? Is it because of the tone used to respond to your contribution? What were you expecting, and why did it not happen? Do you wish you were given more time to explain your idea? Or was it that you didn't speak out and allowed a lesser idea to pass?

The best way to process your feelings is to ask yourself questions and respond to them truthfully in the privacy of your journal. If you do so, you might find your responses startling, but the most important thing is that they will be eye-opening and provide you with invaluable information.

Your initial entries need not necessarily include solutions, such as "I think there is something worrying dad, I should have lunch with him tomorrow." Ideally, start at the problem and then think of various solutions. What's the best way to approach him? Should I speak with someone else close to him first? Why did I think he was worried in the first place?

Hopefully we are starting to show you that there are a variety of ways you can approach your feelings, observations and emotions. Writing like this means you will get to better understand yourself, make better decisions, be more at peace with your difficulties, appreciate things and ultimately add richness to your life.

Handling The First Week

Now that we have visualized what writing regularly in your journal can be like, let us look at how you can try this out—this is the very first week of your journaling venture!

Take a note of the day you start (e.g., Saturday) and schedule some time with yourself in a week to look back over your first week (e.g., next Saturday). An hour or perhaps two hours if you can spare them. You will need some extra time on that day to answer some questions from this book, so it is best if you block out that time now. This will help you get the most out of this experiment and give yourself the opportunity to reflect on how it is going.

What Happened Each Day

For the first week, it is okay if this feels a little alien or robotic—this is perfectly normal when you are starting something new. Plainly write what happened throughout the day. Who you met, what you spoke about, what you did, what you submitted, when you woke up, when you decided to sleep, that work/school assignment you submitted and the feedback, how you felt about a certain interaction, what you wish you should have or need to do going forward, your overall mood for the day, and so on.

Basically, jot down some things that happen each day. Never mind about the structure. Let it be as spontaneous and random as possible. Do not limit yourself—you have enough space to write everything down. So go all out and record whatever you remember from your day or write anything you think you should as the day progresses. But also do not feel under pressure to write a lot if there is not much to say that day. Are you remembering what happened during the day as you settle down for supper or are you filling your journal on the go? Notice when you are finding it is the most natural time for your journaling.

Feelings, Emotions And Opinions

As you go along, it is highly recommended that you make a point to write down your feelings, how did the day as a whole feel. Inspiring? Frustrating? But do not stop there, add a few lines about how specific interactions, events or decisions made you feel.

Take it easy and bullet point any feelings that come to mind if you want to stick to short-form or go all out and explain your feelings in detail if that feels right—you might even find drawing a picture or a doodle useful.

Did you express your opinions or did you chicken out? Or was your opinion severely challenged and you had to rethink it? Are there characters during this day that made you feel unworthy or unprepared, or boosted your confidence? What made you really happy, encouraged, enraged, sad, feel pity, hopeful or dejected, stirred something new or reinforced something you were yet to verbalize? Do not leave anything hanging, pour your heart out on paper.

For some of you, emotions might flow naturally and be the main focus of your journal. Your journal may be full to the brim with feelings and drawings. For others, you might want to write down the events of the day first and *then* take a moment to pause and ask yourself how these events made you feel. You could do this at the same time or a bit later.

Sometimes it is also easier to reflect on something that happened yesterday or a few days ago than knowing how you feel right away. In this case, you might find it useful to read over the last few pages of your journal while figuring out your feelings and opinions about what happened.

At the End of The Week

It has been a whole seven days of journaling so far. You wrote what happened every day (or some days) and recorded whatever you felt and thought about the many things that happened.

You have made it through to Saturday again (if this was your day). A complete week. What do you need to do? In addition to writing about today as normal, read your entries from this week and reflect on them. Answer these questions for as long as you have time today. There are two parts to this:

- How do I feel about the things I have written for the past seven days?
- How does it make me feel to have written something about my life every day (or however frequently) for the last seven days?

You might also want to look back at your initial reasons for journaling.

Do You Notice Anything?

Now, having reviewed your first week, you need to ask yourself the above question. What have you noticed? Remember, you are just getting started with journaling—writing for yourself—so don't expect to already have a long list of insights.

For example, at the end of Week 1 you might have written one or two things along the lines of these examples:

- "Journaling is kind of forcing me to think about my emotions . . . I didn't know I cared/worried this much about this assignment/how I look/what my parents think/what's happening in my community"
- "I find it hard to journal in the morning but I look forward to it as an evening activity"
- "This week I felt my mood change / I had ups and downs"
- "Burning incense isn't for me"
- "From my entries, I now realize I have never really questioned my fitness/what I eat/my friendship group at all"
- "By taking time out each day to journal, I finally realize what '*me time*' is!"
- "I want to try some thicker paper as my pens are bleeding through"
- "I find this really hard and it makes me feel stupid"
- "On Tuesday my mind was blank but for the rest of the week I ran out of time because I had so much to write"

- "I want to buy a small book to carry around with me so I can jot down any thoughts or feelings as they come up"

Writing for yourself is all about self-discovery—learning more about yourself beyond what your bosses, parents, friends, teachers or parents tell you. For many of us, it is a moment of taking back control and making choices and other decisions based on what we truly want rather than what seems to be correct. It is in no way about being perfect, but it can help us come to terms with our imperfections, our biases, weaknesses, and with consistency, we are able to come up with strategies that can reduce our chances of falling for the demands of others that do not necessarily work for us.

At the end of your first week, you are starting the habit of tracking the journaling itself and seeing what it does for *you*. In Chapter 7 we will continue our weekly journaling and introduce some other types of journaling you might want to try out as you are building your new habit. You can move onto this now, or after a few more weeks of writing and tracking how it is going for you.

7

WRITING A LITTLE EVERY DAY

*J*ournaling is likened to having your own therapist on a retainer and is recommended for everyone. It will help you in expressing yourself better, self-evaluate and create a valuable record of your life.

Here is what organizational psychologist, Dr. Benjamin Hardy, and author of *Willpower Doesn't Work* says of his habit of journaling every day.

> *"Journaling daily is the most potent and powerful keystone habit you can acquire. If done correctly, you will show up better in every area of your life — every area! Without question, journaling has by far been the number one factor to everything I've done well in my life."*
>
> — HARDY, 2019

Getting your thoughts from your head to paper every so

often enables a chance to process them more effectively than say, ruminating over them in your mind over the train ride home. You are better placed to remember tasks, identify patterns and derive meaning from what you are thinking about.

American entrepreneur and author Jim Rohn, once said, "*A life worth living is a life worth recording.*" But beyond just recording, a journal can be a useful tool to examine your current life situation, where you want to go as well as appreciate what is going well.

The following sections present several more journaling ideas that can help you write a little every day. You can choose one and stick with it or combine any of them to turn journaling into a daily habit. We mix this up with additional exercises to help you with your reflections.

JOURNAL ABOUT THREE THINGS YOU ARE GRATEFUL FOR

Did you know you can significantly increase your happiness by listing daily the things you are thankful for? A simple habit of taking a moment to reflect on what you are grateful for can help you lead a happier, more content life.

Getting into the habit of recording the positive aspects of your life has been associated with better sleep, less stress, higher levels of happiness, increased self-awareness and generally better health.

A study published in the International Journal for the Advancement of Counselling on the effects of gratitude journaling on Turkish first-year students found that students who kept journals had better levels of adjustment to university life, positive emotions and life satisfaction (Işık & Ergüner-Tekinalp, 2017) compared to those who did not keep one.

As a beginner journaler, the gratitude journal can be a simple way of starting off your journey and setting yourself up for success. You can easily write daily in a gratitude journal as it is a brief and pleasurable activity. You might also choose, for example, to add this on as an evening ritual to your usual habit of writing as you go during the day.

So what is gratitude?

It can be seen as both a state—as in when you recognize the positive outcomes of the actions of others—and a trait—a virtue or a characteristic of an individual to tend to recognize and appreciate the positives of a situation. Some people describe it as more of a "practice" because it is a way of living that you make a choice to follow each day and it is not always easy.

A person practicing gratitude will tend to stimulate happy thoughts from within themselves. They notice the good things in their life and savor small pleasures. They also recognize the sources of the good things, and build up a trust that those good things will often come, whether from actual people or life (or the universe) itself.

Keeping a gratitude journal can be summed up as literally counting your blessings. Our brain is wired to notice risk, danger and potentially negative situations—this is how we have stayed alive as a species this long. These traits are not as useful in the modern world and can bias us toward the negatives of a situation. By regularly writing down and reflecting on a few things you are grateful for, you are rewiring yourself to be paying more attention to the positives in your life. This can help you balance out your everyday experience and build extra resilience in the long run.

There are dozens of gratitude journals to choose from, but the format is less important than how you use it. Some prefer a list style where they make short entries in lists, while others are happy diving deeper with longer posts. You do not have to do the same thing every day.

Many find it a very easy habit to keep up with daily. After some time, you realize you have built a bank of feel-good material that you can refer back to in case you need to drive away some negative emotions. Some people also believe that by practicing gratitude every day you are more likely to see (and grab!) positive opportunities as they pass you by. So, in this way, gratitude can also be linked to success.

WRITE DOWN YOUR DAILY GOALS

A goal-setting study led by Gail Matthews, a psychology professor at the Dominican University in California, found that if you write your goals down, you are 42% more likely to achieve them (Gardner & Albee 2015).

But what exactly does writing them down entail? If you are like Grant Cardone, the author of The 10X Rule, that could mean as much as twice a day (Cardone, n.d.). Here is how he puts it.

> *"I want to wake up to it. I want to go to sleep on it, and I want to dream with it . . . I want to write my goals down before I go to sleep at night because they are important to me, they are valuable to me and I get to wake up to them again tomorrow."*

Journaling about your goals regularly does not only help you remember them, but also helps focus your mind on what is truly important in your life. You get more clarity on what you want to achieve by defining the goals and putting them into words, but importantly, journaling also acts as a motivating factor to do what is necessary to succeed with them.

There is something about writing your goals down that forces you to strategize, measure your progress and explore potential plans of action. Your brain nudges you to take action until your objective is met. If your actions are going against meeting your goal, you will feel uncomfortable. This is your mind sending you a warning shot that you are heading off course—and you can course correct.

It is advisable that you vividly describe your goals—including in pictures or drawings if possible—such that if you show someone else, they can tell exactly what you are trying to achieve. Also, to imagine what it would feel like if you succeeded at each goal. This is associated with a higher chance of goal success.

You do not have to journal about your goals twice a day like Cardone above, but regularly doing so can be very beneficial. Here is a suggestion that you can consider to help you tap into your goals:

- Before your day starts, every morning, write your biggest 5–10 goals on a new page
- The following day, do the same and don't look at the previous day's entries
- Repeat for 30 days and then review

You will find that your goals will be clearer, they might have evolved or changed completely. This habit can be very fulfilling as it keeps reinforcing what is important to you at the moment, what you have achieved already and how you are changing. The number of goals per entry and the frequency is totally up to you.

KEEP A DAILY LOG

If you don't have a specific focus for your journaling, and you don't have much time, then you could try starting with a daily log. There is a good chance you will find topics naturally if you journal about the day-to-day. In log form, you can keep this brief rather than writing at length. Log anything you feel like from what you ate, who you met, what you did to who you spoke to.

KEEP A "BEST THING TODAY" JOURNAL

This is another habit that can easily help you grow into regular journaling without causing you to feel overwhelmed and that you lack content to put down.

It is as simple as choosing just one thing that you consider was the very best thing that happened in your day. You answer the question, "What is the best thing that happened today?" Focus on one thing to write about rather than everything that went well or that you are grateful for today. Do this at the end of the day just before going to sleep to bring your day to a positive and uplifting close.

You can have a small separate journal for this purpose or it can also be part of your regular journal. It could also be the first, or only journal you keep. The answer to the question can be one line or several paragraphs, but try to concentrate on that one "best" thing. For best results, do it right before going to bed. You can write it while in bed too, just before your turn off the lights.

JOURNAL ON A CALENDAR

To spur your journaling habit and make it as simple as possible while keeping yourself accountable, you can choose to write on a calendar rather than a notebook.

Get yourself a sizable desk calendar or planner and commit to writing one or two sentences each day about the day you have had. You have the freedom to choose whatever topics are important to you including goals, gratitude or simply a log of what happened that day.

This is a good starting point since the amount of writing required of you is fairly little and quite achievable. A desk calendar might not be portable. A planner, however, can be carried around when you have to spend days away from the house.

What makes this approach even better is the fact that the calendar has an accountability effect since you cannot avoid noticing the fact that you have skipped a day or two. As you build up the habit, you will find the calendar a very useful motivating factor to taking a little time of your day to reflect on and document your life.

CREATE A TEMPLATE (NEXT LEVEL JOURNAL PROMPTS)

One of the challenges to consistently writing a journal are moments when you stare at a blank page and think, "I don't know what to write today!"

You can spare yourself these moments by creating a template

that you can always follow. One that captures your initial or current reasons for starting to journal.

If you have preferred the more structured approach so far and have been collecting journal prompts, the template could be a year-long collection of writing prompts. By pre-picking a prompt for each day or randomly from an idea jar, you can make this into a whole month or year template. One such example of a prompt is, "You are locked in a room with your greatest fear. Describe what is in the room."

It could also incorporate aspects of the gratitude journal, writing three things you feel grateful for every evening or responding to one or more questions that help you reflect such as, "What can I do to make tomorrow better than today?" or "What could I have done differently today?" This aspect could be the same every day, whereas the prompts are changing.

You can never go wrong with lists. You can have so much fun with all kinds of lists without running into the brick wall of not finding something to write about. For example, "5 things I love," "3 things I learned today," "7 things I must try," or "My funniest childhood memories." Another useful feature to consider adding to a template is open-ended prompts that you can turn into lists of whatever length, allowing you to review your evolving responses over time. For example, "It was great that . . .", "It will be great when . . .", "Wouldn't it be nice if . . ." and so on.

You can even design the template on Microsoft Word, print it out into journaling worksheets, then bind them together—creating your own journal.

Most importantly, if you take time to initially create a template, it could be a sure way of never running out of something to write about. It doesn't have to be static, either. Amend it as you please and by all means, make it fun!

Keeping a daily journal is in many ways a big decision to make. And besides this one decision, our lives involve hundreds if not thousands of decisions—some conscious and others unconscious. Journaling itself can help you make decisions. You could even choose to keep a decision journal.

REFLECTING ON YOUR DECISION MAKING

You are the sum total of your decisions. Your success or failure is based heavily on the decisions you make throughout your life. Bear in mind also that your decisions and actions are primarily based on the goals that you have set for yourself. There is no other way around it unless you want to rely on luck.

Decision making is a critical and inevitable aspect of our existence. Your journal can be a very useful tool in aiding you to make life decisions. You can save yourself the mental overload, wander, fears and many other difficult experiences associated with making decisions.

We sometimes depend on our bosses, teachers, peers or parents to help us come up with solutions, make decisions or just aid us in improving our decision-making. But they are not always available to help or steer us. They will also be making the decision from their own opinions and life experiences. Often a decision will only be right for us if we make it ourselves and follow our own path. The journey will have ups and downs and twists and turns, but we will be following our own unique path through these events rather than someone else's idea of how it should be done. We can learn and adjust our course as we go—in a way that suits us as an individual.

One of the best ways to really get better at decision making is to pay particular attention to the process through which we end up making them—testing the process. Princeton University psychologist and Nobel prize–winning economist Daniel Kahneman says that decision journaling is one of the best ways to take over control of your decision-making process.

He argues that by writing about the decisions we make, we are able to do away with what he calls *hindsight bias*—our tendency to look back at our decision-making processes with a lens that is most favorable to us. Such that we can explain every outcome without learning from our mistakes (Baer, 2013).

By recording our decision-making process, we are able to maintain honest and accurate feedback of what exactly we were thinking while making the decision. We are then able to better determine if we were ignorant but lucky or smart but unlucky, which is good practice for better decision-making in the future.

Here is how it works. Since we already have a record of what we expected to happen and why we thought it would be so, we can actually tell if our decision-making process was right and take this on board for future decisions. Contrast that with having no written record of your decision making. Our default setting is to believe that what we predict will come true—but writing it down means we have an accurate account of what actually happened for each belief that we held.

Now, journaling about your decisions will not necessarily be a daily event. You might want to reserve it for decisions that are significant. When doing this, consider the following:

- When making a decision that you consider big or

consequential, take some time out to think and write down your expectations.
- Add why you expect the specific outcome you envision.
- Write also how you are feeling about that situation, emotionally and physically.
- Do you feel confused, tired, confident or drained?
- Are there any trade-offs or alternatives?
- Avoid using ambiguous language; use simple words and be very clear.

You also stand a chance at recognizing holes in your decision when you are first making it and writing it down. Your brain is forced to analyze it and if something doesn't seem right, you are compelled to rethink it.

Review your decision journal after each major decision and every few months. It is part of the process to better your decision-making. Take stock of the mistakes you made and how you made them. You can tell what kind of decisions you are good or bad at. If you have a mentor or coach, you can review your decisions with them and further help you identify what to improve on.

There is a science to decision making; coming up with a defined process, optimizing for time and quality and articulating the decision. It can be pretty exhausting being in the driver's seat for that long. Research shows that as we make more decisions, the quality decreases since we simply get more tired. By reviewing your decision-making journal regularly, you can improve and make the process of handling tough decisions less taxing.

FOCUS ON BUILDING YOUR AUTHENTICITY

One of the advantages of journaling as we mentioned earlier is *introducing yourself to your true self.* I know that may sound a little cheesy to some of us, but if you look at the screen-obsessed world we live in, with a work life characterized by quick meetings and email, you may recognize that being your true self feels riskier than ever before.

In one way or another, we are either consciously or subconsciously trying to fit in, be accepted and liked. The personas we present, especially on social media, are often the versions of ourselves we would like the world to see and not really who we are.

This is even more pronounced in our younger years—teenage, college life and during entry-level phases of our careers. Typically, without as much conscious effort, when we are better grounded in our career and life paths, we will tend to be less uneasy about our public portrayals. That is not to say that even in our 30s, 40s and beyond, we cannot be held hostage by the need to appear perfect or suffer from impostor syndrome—which means having chronic self-doubt despite evident or enviable success—but it is less likely.

> *"By being someone you are not, you are telling yourself that who you really are isn't okay. So hiding or suppressing who you really are can end up leaving you feeling lonely, disconnected from others, or even worthless."*
>
> — DR. TCHIKI DAVIS, THE FOUNDER OF BERKELEY WELL-BEING INSTITUTE

WHAT IS AUTHENTICITY?

Dr. Tchiki says authenticity or being authentic is a character trait that means you are always *showing your true self and how you feel*. Expressing your whole self in a genuine way rather than only presenting a particular version of yourself. To be truly authentic, then you have to first know who you truly are. What better way to get there than daily journaling about *you*?

In the technology age we live in, it is understandably harder to be our true selves; we consume a lot of media products that subliminally attempt to dictate to us what we should be, should want and even how to express ourselves. And we will often fall prey to these popular versions of the "ideal" human being.

Our loss of authenticity cannot be fairly blamed only on the media. It has a lot to do with our upbringing—our teachers, peers, parents, religions and the society we grew up around largely shaped who we became. So, for many of us, there is a huge pressure to maintain the emotions, beliefs, behaviors and thoughts that align with what we were taught. Even if at this point in time, they do not work so well for us anymore.

Even with more awareness of our own values, we are still uneasy—something best summed up in the literary work of one of the most widely read African novelists, Chinua Achebe—*No Longer At Ease*, a sequel to the more popular *Things Fall Apart*. It depicts the tragic life of Obi Okonkwo, a British-educated man in pre-independence Nigeria who is torn between preserving the values and customs of pre-colonial Nigeria and the demands of his "modern European job" whose ethics he can't help but find repulsive (Achebe, 1994).

Like Obi, we are often trying to balance between the outer

and inner aspects of ourselves for the purposes of fitting in, finding love, or achieving success in line with the rules of an ever changing world. That "modern" world that we strive so hard to fit in or "find our place in" can also be very superficial, define success in terms of the dollars in our bank accounts and perfection rather than how true we are to our values.

The authentic person ideally strives to earn respect through what they have to contribute to society while being who they truly are. Now, that journey begins with an urge to know what their purpose is and live it. To do that you have to consciously find the deeper meaning of your life and crave the fulfillment that comes with being truly yourself—being authentic. If you are even remotely inspired to uncover your authentic self and live by it, journaling for your authentic self is the way to go.

It will also crucially help you build a unique voice for yourself, say, in negotiations, as a writer or as a leader in any capacity: are you a school captain, the president of a students' association, a product, line or general manager, the leader figure in your family or a community group? Authenticity journaling will help you become more believable, relatable and persuasive. You are able to develop your own voice—the distinct personality, point of view, and style that not only identifies you but also is satisfying every time you stay true to yourself.

JOURNALING FOR AUTHENTICITY

All journaling helps build authenticity. By trying out the exercises thus far in this book, you have actually already started—and you didn't know it! A bonus gift from us! If you want to travel further on this self-discovery journey, you could make a guided journal specifically focusing on authenticity—meaning, you create a template with relevant prompts to help you find yourself. We have included some examples below to get you started:

- Given the ability to drastically change your life, would you do it? And how?
- In what 5 ways are you living your life to fulfill the expectations of others?
- What brings you joy? Are your actions in alignment with that?
- If money wasn't a problem, how would you be spending your time?
- When do you feel like you are being held back by others? If you needed to break free, how would you do it?
- How have you changed yourself to gain acceptance from others?
- If no one else was watching, what activity would you love doing?
- What would you try if you knew you could not fail?

That is where regular journaling comes into play. You will have a record of who you truly want to be in specific written words and scenarios, and even when you encounter something entirely new, writing about it will help you determine if you bowed to external pressure and why, or if you remained authentic. You can ask yourself questions like: did it hurt me or others? What was the opportunity cost? If I was in a similar situation again, would I have stood my ground as I did?

There is a lot of joy in being your authentic self. It will take honesty and strength in this journaling process and a commitment to acknowledging external interference, when you feel the urge to please others rather than remain truthful to yourself. You will also realize that you won't get to a specific point where you'll have achieved authenticity and stop, but rather, you will come to practice it your whole life —and it will be worth every minute. You will not have a conflict of conscience.

REVIEWING YOUR WEEK

Over time, you will likely find that you have more thoughts and ideas at the end of each week about your life and about how your journaling project is going. Here are some prompts that might help you think about this in more detail than you did in your first weeks:

- Was it hard to stay consistent?
- Did you miss some days?
- Did it drain you?
- What did you forget to record?
- Can you keep doing this?
- Do you think you will achieve your objectives?
- Did you remain true to the reason you wanted to start journaling?
- Should you try doing it differently? Or, do you want to give up now?

Look back at the reasons you wanted to start journaling. Expecting instant results is a recipe for failure but reviewing your progress regularly will more likely lead you to your desired outcome. Seeing how your feelings are changing (or not changing) over time can help you get a sense of whether your overall situation has improved, stayed the same or worsened. You can also see how much progress you have made in terms of your goals by reading over your entries.

EVERY NOW AND AGAIN

You might want to schedule some special time every now and again to journal. This is an extension of the idea of looking back over your week, but you are looking back over a longer period. You could also use the time to treat yourself to a longer journaling session without worrying about the time or the next thing on your to-do list. You could even bring some self-care practices into your journaling session. This offers a special time to review as well as keeping your overall journaling project exciting.

For example, once every few weeks when you feel really exhausted, choose an evening to take a bubble bath, wrap yourself in a robe and for an hour do nothing else but journal. You could make this a special treat that you give yourself every month, every term or every quarter—or there might be a meaningful date that you would like to take some time out to reflect on like an anniversary.

Some people like to reflect on the time that has passed—whether that's the financial quarter in their job or looking back at the season in their life that has just finished. Other aspects from nature that can be used by journalers are setting goals by the new moon and reflecting on progress every full moon. It is a personal choice what time period is meaningful and how often you would like to schedule these extra special activities.

In summary, we have talked about how you can help yourself to become a more authentic person by regular journaling.

There are so many individual and combined ways to ensure

that you can write in your journal regularly without feeling overwhelmed, still keeping it fun and worth looking forward to. We hope that you find a way that fits for you from the ideas that we have given in Chapters 4 through 7.

When you need to, utilize the easy entry points such as guided journals/templates or writing one line a day. This way, you will always have something to write about, and writing a little every day won't feel like a chore. Plus then your habit will not dry up completely if you fall off the wagon for a few days.

Feel free to experiment, tweak and overhaul your journaling process at any point until it fits your schedule, personality and goals. In fact, how fun would it be if your journal was never on a static structure? You will have the opportunity to reflect on how your journaling is going again in Chapter 9 when we consider the literature on forming habits. We recommend you spend anywhere from a few weeks up to three months continuing your journaling before you read more about that in Chapter 9.

Chapter 8 is a standalone chapter about using journaling to help empty your mind when it is busy. You can try this at any point or you might have already read it when you started.

8

STOP! WRITING THINGS DOWN WHEN YOUR MIND IS BUSY

*H*ave you ever thought about how long your heart has been beating? It is not really something we would normally ask ourselves or even be conscious of, unless, perhaps, if we end up in the hospital or another health-related trauma reminds us of how fragile life is.

But to answer this question, about five weeks into a pregnancy, the heartbeat of a fetus is detectable. It is about the same time that the brain starts developing (McDonald, 2019). Without venturing any further into the medical field, we can say that your brain has worked for longer than you can remember.

For some of us, sitting still for just ten minutes is quite difficult. We have to always seek something to keep us engaged. We feel that we have always got to be doing something. Watching a movie? We might still want to scroll through our phones at the same time to keep our minds fully occupied. Seeking constant stimulation to keep boredom at bay could mean we are never really able to relax and silence our minds. It might also be that we are using this stimulation to keep us distracted from a worry, something painful or difficult, which can be very tiring to keep up as a way of coping with that worry.

Either way, your brain is barely able to shut off. Instead, it could wander from one place to another randomly. It is no surprise that you then begin worrying about something else that five minutes ago was not an issue, and on and on . . .

RACING THOUGHTS

These are described as fast, often-worrying thoughts about a particular topic that typically become repetitive. They come in an array of forms including financial, health, phobias, "what ifs" and embarrassing topics in single or multiple lines of thought. These thoughts are often associated with anxiety or stress. Below is an example presented by Dr. Patricia Harteneck, a senior psychologist at New York's Seleni Institute.

> *"I always forget what I have to do. I'm so stupid. If I don't remember everything, I'll get fired. I don't know what I'll do if that happens. I should have taken that job I was offered six months ago. If I lose my job, I won't have any money. I need to work longer hours to keep this job. That just makes me more depressed. I'm so miserable. What am I going to do?"*

Racing thoughts could be replays of events that happened in the past that made you anxious or sad. They could also be a string of worries about things that may happen in the future. But they are often blown out of proportion, consume productive time, follow a certain repeating pattern and are unlikely to come to a satisfactory conclusion.

If such kinds of thoughts occupy your mind, your energy is severely drained. Instead of living in the present, you could be stuck in an endless loop in your brain that is hard to escape. Concentration and even the ability to complete regular daily tasks can be affected, as is your sleep and memory.

If you do get to a point where you feel you need more support than this book can offer, then we have included some suggested resources in the appendix, which we hope are useful.

WORRYING

We can sum up all the above with the word *worry*. It would be a lie to say that you can truly kick worry out of your life. We all worry. But if it goes on for too long, it will potentially reduce productivity on top of taking away your peace of mind.

No one, absolutely no one is immune to worrying. It could get the better of anyone. Private concerns, work issues, school stresses and in some cases some irrational thoughts—these all can occupy your brain until you lose the ability to perform everyday tasks as you normally would.

Stopping the worries is never an easy task. When your mind is filled with these racing thoughts and worries, journaling can seem like a very difficult undertaking. However, the good news is that journaling can offer an effective way of quieting these thoughts and allowing your mind to focus on the present. So, how do you free your mind from these thoughts and focus on what is important to you?

STOP, SLOW DOWN AND REFOCUS

A busy mind forces you to not fully focus on the moment that you are living in. It is filled with unruly thoughts and untamed emotions that put your attention everywhere else but on the *now*. Thought after thought, fears, doubts and emotions are churned out, creating a sea of clutter and chaos that you cannot really swim through.

This is in no way strange, unusual or unique to you. It happens to everyone. We constantly operate with a lot of mental noise: plans, analysis, judgments, forecasts, comments, memories and so on, enough to keep you awake at night. This mental junk, distraction and drama drains and leaves us exhausted. Sometimes the only moment we realize how much our busy lives affect us is when we collapse on our beds at the end of the day.

That is why it is important to pause and clear our minds of the clutter—to completely empty our mind of all the stuff that is keeping us from focusing on the present. Journaling is one of the most effective ways of doing this.

While we will all experience moments where our thinking is clouded by a huge amount of thoughts that we cannot really process at once, we will experience this at different times and intensities, unique to our situations. It could be at any time of the day regardless of what we are doing; interesting lectures, just after a job interview, before a major presentation, or even during a *normal* day when we are not making any major decisions or having to fight from our corner.

This is something a portable journal works well for. Feeling foggy or anxious? Find a quiet place, take out your journal and just empty everything that is getting you disoriented onto paper. Write freely, do not try to follow any format or try to make any corrections, aesthetic or otherwise—simply unload your brain. After writing down everything that seems to be bothering you, figure out what is the most pressing issue and analyze it. If you can come up with a point of action now, write it down and implement it. But the mere fact that you have written down what is filling your mind allows you to ease pressure on yourself, and you can better focus on the moment.

Write down your thoughts and be as expressive as you can. Get down to the details, e.g., "I feel frustrated because . . .", "I just can't seem to focus. During the meeting, I kept thinking about yesterday evening and how I mistakenly . . ." and so on. When you have these thoughts in writing, there is a calming effect that you achieve, since the things overloading your brain have cleared. You are also more likely to be able to pinpoint your greatest concerns. You stand a better chance at deciding what can wait for later and that which needs to be handled right there and then.

Creating regular time is often not necessary or useful for this type of journaling. This is more a practical response when your brain fog or loud chatter is so much that it can't wait. It really depends on how urgent decluttering feels for you at that time.

At the end of the day, even if our daytime experience was not so messy, our brain can feel like it speeds up at night. As the rest of our body slows down, it can allow the space for thoughts to pop up that we were not aware of during the day. If this is true for you, it can help to build a ritual of emptying your brain of all worries, indecisions, conflicts before going to bed—or have a journal ready for the nights that the thoughts rise up.

You can clear your mind before going to bed by not only

writing down your thoughts and feelings, but also analyzing them to find solutions, create actions points and possibly come up with a priority list. Ending the day with a clearer mind and even just a few solutions to work on tomorrow can help you have a more peaceful sleep and guarantee additional energy to handle the challenges of the next day.

SLEEP AND JOURNALING

Just how important is sleep?

Let us first consider one of the things considered most essential for a healthy body—food. Say you were marooned on a desert island and couldn't find food for a few days, how would it feel? Chances are that you would feel pretty uncomfortable, surely very hungry, weak and would lose some weight. However, you would likely survive for up to a few weeks, as long as you found some water early on in your ordeal.

Clinical trials analyzed by the American Association for the Advancement of Science have even backed up claims that there are health advantages to cutting back on food five days each month, such as in the prevention and treatment of age-related ailments, including heart disease and diabetes (Leslie, 2017).

Depriving yourself of sleep for a similar number of days, however, is a totally different case. Here is a possible timeline of the effects of sleep deprivation:

- **24 hours**: According to the Centers for Disease Control and Prevention (CDC), staying awake for at least 24 hours is equivalent to having a Blood Alcohol Content of 0.10%, which is higher than the legal limit in all US states (0.08%). Symptoms exhibited after 24 hours may include: drowsiness, irritability, decreased alertness and concentration, issues with coordination, brain fog, puffy eyes and fatigue.

- **36 hours**: The symptoms intensify as well as the urge to sleep and incidents of *microsleeps*—brief periods of involuntary sleep lasting up to 30 minutes. Symptoms may include: slow reaction time, impaired decision-making, increased errors, impaired memory, difficulty learning new information, behavioral changes and difficulties processing social cues.
- **48 hours**: This is now called "extreme" sleep deprivation, where it is harder to stay awake and chances of having *microsleeps* are much higher. You could even start hallucinating. Effects may include: anxiety, increased irritability, heightened stress levels, extreme fatigue and depersonalization (a sense of detachment from your own identity, a dreamlike state).
- **72 hours**: Longer and more frequent *microsleeps*, longer and more detailed hallucinations, impaired perception, delusions and disordered thinking are possible effects.
- **96 hours**: 4 days awake and you will likely have a severely distorted perception of reality and an incredible urge to sleep.

From this comparison only, you could say—for argument's sake—that sleep seems to be more important than food. Or to be a little more accurate, daily sleep is more important than daily food.

This may be different for every individual, but sleep deprivation is such a serious issue that Amnesty International recognizes it as a form of torture (SMH, 2006).

You might think that this does not apply to you, but consider the American working culture. More often than not pulling long working hours is associated and even celebrated as a requisite for high performance and vitality. A "dedicated" manager could clock an 80-hour work week, a Wall Street trader could sleep at midnight and wake up at 2:30 a.m. to check market opening activity, a PhD student endures shifting sleeping patterns, and barely any sleep for months ahead of the hard deadline.

In fact, a 2016 CDC study found that one in three adult Americans were not getting enough sleep on a regular basis (CDC, 2016). The American Sleep Apnea association further estimates that between 50 and 70 million Americans of all ages and socioeconomic classes are affected by sleep-related problems. If you are wondering what the ideal amount of sleep time to aim for is, the Sleep Research Society and the American Academy of Sleep Medicine recommend a minimum of 7 hours for adults (18–60). Teens should get at least 8–10 hours of sleep while for school-age children, 9–12 hours of sleep each night is recommended.

Getting enough sleep is associated with overall good health. This includes:

- a healthy weight
- a lower risk of serious health conditions such as diabetes or heart disease
- lower blood pressure and reduced stress
- better memory, thinking more clearly and better decision-making

- better performance at school and productivity at work
- improved immune function, as well as
- better emotional and social interactions along with improved mood.

Insufficient sleep takes away all of these advantages.

HOW DOES JOURNALING HELP

If you find you are having trouble sleeping, the US department of Health and Human Services recommends that you keep a sleep diary, one of the best ways to keep track of your sleep patterns. You can then share it with your doctor before trying to use over-the-counter sleep medicine.

You would track some data for analysis, for example:

- I slept at ___ and woke up at ___
- My last meal was ___ at ___ time
- The season is ___ [Winter/Summer] and I slept at ___
- How tired you were at/after work
- Last drink before sleep (water/alcohol/caffeine) ___ plus any smoking?
- Any exercises done?
- Did you take any medications?

While a sleeping diary is very important to help your doctor make a proper diagnosis, it may not necessarily help you achieve better sleep. But journaling could. Here are a few ways how journaling could help.

WORRY

Whether your working hours are eating into your sleep or not, one of the biggest documented causes of poor sleep is worry.

Worry will keep you awake. The inability to cease thinking about a work project, a school assignment, unpaid bills, something you regret, any of those whirring thoughts. Your mind is racing to a point where you feel you cannot control them—"I need to do this, and that . . . oh, I forgot this . . . next week/month I need to . . . oh why aren't I asleep yet?! . . . I'm going to be so tired tomorrow!" Before you know it an hour or two has gone by without you falling asleep.

But what if you wrote those thoughts down, instead of thinking deeply about them under your sheets with the lights off? You can slow down, achieve some calmness and put your most urgent challenges in perspective. That is what journaling does for you—it allows you to get into a deeper level of processing.

> *"One of the biggest barriers to falling asleep for people is that we have thoughts circling around in our heads when we turn out the lights. These thought processes work in opposition to relaxing and falling asleep."*
>
> — DR. MICHAEL SCULLIN, ASSISTANT PROFESSOR OF PSYCHOLOGY AND NEUROSCIENCE AT BAYLOR UNIVERSITY.

The point is not mere journaling, but what you journal about when worries prevent you from sleeping. A growing body of research finds that offloading your worries just before bed can help reduce worry and anxiety.

A study published in the Journal of Experimental Psychology sums up what is now becoming a consensus: that writing down a to-do list just before bed can help you fall asleep faster than journaling about all you have accomplished (Scullin et al., 2018). The researchers also found that the more specific your entries get, the faster you fall asleep.

These studies challenge what would be our instinctive assumption that by writing all you have accomplished, you are patting yourself on the back and are therefore less worried, and writing about what needs to be accomplished would make us more worried about them. It turns out this is not the case.

As such, penning down everything that we are worrying about or trying to remember (the to-do list), all organized in one place from which you can pick it up the next day, helps you relax, put your mind at ease and get to sleep.

And you do not have to do this for long. Researchers find just five minutes is enough—you may just be jotting down some bullet notes for tomorrow. However, if you feel you need longer on some days, it is worth spending the time to unload everything from your mind until it feels lighter.

A WORRY JOURNAL

If you turn the lights off and get between your sheets while you are worried about the things you have to do tomorrow, or pondering other anxious thoughts, there is a big chance that sleep will prove elusive.

Your anxiety will effectively be injecting cortisol—our primary stress hormone that acts as a stimulant—into your system. It's like having a couple of coffees before sleep, and can be the driver behind your toss and turns when you are worried. Too much cortisol in your bloodstream can affect you in the short term (acute stress) and the longer term as well (chronic stress).

In such situations, the worry journal can be your savior. This is an emotional outlet where you put down, freely, all your daily anxieties. You're basically putting your worries somewhere else away from your mind and freeing you to sleep. You might want to call this something else like a "brain dump, "mind drawer," or "thought bucket"—whatever is meaningful to you. Anything that helps you give yourself permission to put those thoughts down for the night. They will be there in the morning, if and when you are ready for them again.

Writing down your worries has been proven to slow down whirring thoughts. They will evaporate into your journal and become less distracting. The simple act of acknowledging your thoughts could make them much easier to process as well as give you some clarity on why they are preventing you from sleeping.

Remember, the worry journal is not all about venting or collating all your negative thoughts. It will be much less effective if you do not try to come up with a plan. Try considering the probability of these fears actually happening. If they actually did happen, what would you do to cope?

Now with that, before you go to sleep, you already have a contingency plan. What can you do to prevent them from happening? Can you do it within the period you have determined it could happen? Who can help you in handling this?

You now have everything you can do about that worry and every other worry on your list. So should you really be agonizing over it, or starting tomorrow start taking action on the solutions you gathered?

Not all worries will have a quick response like this, so some of them you are writing down for later—when you might have more energy to find a solution. You may choose to keep them in your drawer or bucket until a few days later. Other things you may need to pick up and put down several times before you have any clarity. You can put them down again each night that you need to.

Here are some tips to consider as you get started with your worry journal:

- **Write your worries down, literally**: Stick to the old-fashioned pen-and-paper approach rather than the screen. The advantages of handwriting something are quite pronounced here. It works best if you want to really download *all* of the thoughts and feelings that are currently whirring round. Remember, you are writing for yourself, so no one cares about your handwriting (or will even ever see it).

Write everything, and remember, it's freewriting. Whatever your grammar teacher said doesn't really have to count, so don't get too self-conscious about your punctuation, for example. Just let your thoughts flow like a river. If you do want to make corrections, you can always do this later.

- **DO NOT worry about the frequency**: How counterproductive would it be if the worry journal would become something in itself to worry about?

So, don't get too bothered that you skipped a day or two. You write in it only on the days you need to, not because you have to every day without fail.

Some days will be enjoyable, but others will have lots of issues that could keep you awake, which is when you need the worry journal.

- **Create some time to journal before you normally want to sleep**: Beginning journaling moments before the time you want to sleep could potentially make you find yourself struggling between drifting off and remembering what you need to "offload." This means the "offloading" part could continue after your head hits the pillow, negating the purpose of the journal. Give yourself adequate time to journal before you go to sleep. Try fifteen minutes to start with and go from there.
- **Always know you have the power**: Inasmuch as we might benefit from the insights of others (our bosses, friends, parents, etc.), you cannot afford to allow someone to dictate how your life goes. We are the ultimate bosses of our lives.

Even when we get insights or advice about our life decisions, we ultimately retain the power to make the final move. Journaling reinforces this—outside counsel is considered in a similar manner as your own ideas. Write your worries down, then your options and possible solutions, and you can determine the course of action to take.

You reassert your control for yourself, come to a resolution or in the least, achieve a new perspective—and gain some peace of mind. Once you release this burden, you are inching closer to some sweet, restful sleep.

- **Guided journaling:** If you find it easier to follow some prompts, here are some below to try out, that relate to sleep and worry;
- I wish today I could have . . .
- Today I should have . . .
- I cannot sleep because I am worrying about . . .
- I cannot sleep because I have this idea about . . .
- I cannot sleep because tomorrow I have . . .
- I cannot sleep because I am still thinking about fixing . . .
- My life feels . . .
- I am still mad about . . .

Remember, guided journaling and the associated prompts helps trigger your thinking in the direction of things that are occupying your brain, helping you express and process them and as such help you get some sleep at the end.

MORE OPTIONS FOR THE BUSY MIND

The to-do list has been endorsed by several studies as one of the most effective methods of journaling for good sleep. We also wanted to include in the book some other hints and tips on sleep that can be used in combination with your journaling.

- If possible, leave your smartphone and other digital devices away from the bedroom, or keep them out of reach by an arm's length. You are setting the scene for sleep. The idea is to reduce distractions and stop you continuing with tasks that will keep you going

at high speed. Try not to start anything new or tune into any new information like a late night news broadcast.
- The hour leading up to sleep is about slowing down. Try taking a few deep breaths before you move onto the next task. Some things can wait until tomorrow. Ask yourself what you could do instead to prepare yourself for sleep?
- Create the right ambience that encourages you to relax. Candles? Soft music or lighting? Essential oil diffusers for aromatherapy? You might use these to have a bath before you journal—or a shower (you can actually drop essential oils into the shower too and get a rush of scented steam instead).

PEACE, CERTAINTY AND ACTION

Remember, not every single thing that you are dealing with today will have a clear answer. Equally, not everything needs to be fixed at the moment. Everything has a timeline. Figuring this out is part of your daily journaling process.

It can help you come up with strategies to solve the most urgent challenges first, where you may need to act soon. This calls for a good level of decision-making; prioritizing, determining resources needed, estimating outcomes, accounting for eventualities and so on. Some worries will need to be revisited at a later date when you have the energy and time to fully dissect them. Other challenges, you may have the energy now, but perhaps the issue needs some time to simmer before you decide or act on it.

Some worries call for you to make a challenge, or rather put up a fight. There are many forms of challenges. Are you challenging your beliefs or are you challenging the authority or circumstances responsible for these worries? This does not necessarily mean a confrontation. Instead, you can work through a critical analysis of what has put you in an uncomfortable situation. It could simply take a table format: on one side the points for, and the other side the points against, in other words, pros and cons. First, write everything you think would make sense for both sides, then read through and make an informed stand. This could also include a third opinion you consider unbiased.

On the other side, you might find it useful to consider the notion of accepting some of the things that cause you sleepless nights or days with a busy mind. We can call it "practicing acceptance"—which is a whole concept in itself—but to get you started, you can try out the following steps:

- **Notice and record your worry/discomfort/anxiety**: Some journaling prompts to consider include, "I can feel myself becoming more and more nervous about . . .", "I am beginning to get worked up about . . .", "I am going to sleep, but . . ."
- **Accept it**: Your discomfort makes sense. You have been visualizing negative outcomes. You are already bracing for the worst case scenario. This is a built-in biological response when you feel threatened and survival mode kicks in. *Accept* that this response will happen to anyone as it is happening to you and that trying to resist it will only make things worse.
- **Use words to support that you accept**: When you make the decision to accept your situation, take it as you would if, for example, someone screamed or shrieked right behind you in a public place but you soon found out it was for a trivial reason like a

prank. You realize that it is no longer and never was an emergency situation. But also be compassionate and understanding that there might still be a lot of nervousness remaining around it, too. Use statements that show your acceptance such as, "It's fine to be nervous," or "It's normal to be anxious in this situation. I know I can handle this feeling."

Accepting your discomfort is the foundation. Compare this with getting worked up as you tell yourself something like, "I need to feel better right now!," "I can't stand this," "This is an emergency!", or "I must stop this now, I'm so weak!"

TIPS TO ACCEPTING YOUR WORRIES

You can view your worries in the following ways to make them less scary, more empowering and to increase your chances of overcoming them:

- **A protective mechanism**: You can view your worries as a signal about what you need. So by recording when and where your worries stem from, you can deduce what your mind is trying to tell you. One fairly straightforward way is keeping you safe as a fight-or-flight mechanism. Basically, your worry could be an indication you are in danger, either physically or a harder to grasp type of emotional danger. Now, with this lens, you could try and figure out what warnings your worries are giving you.
- **Balancing life and work**: Achieving a good work-life balance will give you the ability to experience and enjoy life more fully. A lot of the worries that keep us awake are related to school or work. For

example, we are biting off more than we can chew or, in a sense, we feel we don't have a choice. If we pause to consider which parts of our lives our anxieties and worries belong to, we can think about how we want those pieces to look and work toward living a more balanced life.
- **Is it anxiety or excitement?** I know this might sound counterintuitive, but can you nevertheless try to reframe your worries from "I am worried about . . ." to "I am excited about . . ." You possibly have come across the statement, "Anxiety is excitement without the breath," which means you feel anxious instead of excited because you are not breathing. Taking a breath and considering why you are worried can help transform this feeling and you may discover something else.

Maybe you are not allowing yourself to experience the moment fully because of nervousness. Are you being too fatalistic? As you journal about your feelings, it would not hurt to consider whether you are anxious about that particular thing because it is also very exciting for you. These feelings can actually be quite similar, and choosing to go with excitement can take you a long way.

- **Try turning your worries into motivation**: Worry and motivation are in many ways similar, but the difference is your chosen interpretation. The drive that pushes you forward, the fight-or-flight energy, can be channeled into different things. For example, some people have spoken about turning self-hate into self-honesty and balance—and perfectionism of the self-defeating kind into an artistic vision. Anyone can achieve this for

themselves, and it can all begin with journaling about your worries.
- **A route to dealing with high pressure scenarios:** Calvin McDuffie, a wellness coach, battled severe anxiety from the age of 15. Several prescriptions later, he found a way out for himself. He used what many would have called an *unfortunate situation* as a strength. Having dealt with anxieties for a long time, he realized he coped well in high-pressure environments, something that has propelled him to leadership positions as well as mentorship.

In summary, worries and anxieties are some of the biggest reasons for a clouded mind, or what you might call a busy mind. Whether it is for better sleep or improved decision-making, bringing your most important concerns into perspective begins with writing them down, and then working your way through it. You declutter your mind, find peace and importantly, clear space to tackle problems more efficiently.

HABITS: FORMING THEM AND KEEPING THEM

TAKING STOCK

You have been trying out journaling for a few weeks now or even a few months. If you haven't done so already, you might find it useful to schedule a longer session with yourself (like we discussed at the end of Chapter 7) to look back over your journal entries and ask yourself how it feels to be journaling now after this time.

Now that you have been journaling a while, this chapter introduces some ideas around forming and keeping habits that hopefully you will find useful for your new journaling habit. Is it a habit yet?

INTRODUCTION TO FORMING HABITS

Forming habits can be hard, and maintaining the habits for life can even be harder. Wouldn't it be just nice if our lives could run effectively on autopilot? Imagine if all you had to do was decide what you wanted and it would materialize right away. Your academic and career goals, sleeping patterns, your relationships, fitness, mood, basically anything you wanted.

Unfortunately, life doesn't work like that. Even commercial pilots must manually take off and land—the most important parts of a flight in between the cruising altitude. And what if the autopilot disengages, there is turbulence, or in the unlikely event that onboard computers fail?

You can make things easier for yourself by forming habits. Once something becomes a habit, it is easier to start it and get it done, and you don't need as much energy as when you are first learning how to do it.

For instance, a seasoned airplane pilot doesn't have to remind themselves to conduct a pre-flight inspection. After doing it so many times, it becomes a habit, and it is very unlikely that they would start a flight without performing the pre-flight inspection. Similarly, if you want your journaling journey to be successful, you have to turn journaling into a habit.

Fortunately, forming and maintaining new habits is actually not as hard as it might seem. Unlike what is said of teaching an old dog new tricks, even when we already have developed routines over the years, the difference between your adopting new habits or not comes down to two main reasons:

1. Either you don't have a clear understanding of the structure of habits and how to use it to your advantage, or
2. You are setting yourself up for failure by trying to do too much too soon.

By working through this guide, you have learned a lot about journaling: types of journals, required tools and equipment, what to journal about, advantages of journaling, and so on. This chapter is probably going to be the most important for you so far, since merely knowing how, when and why you need to do something is no guarantee that you will ever do it consistently.

Based on the above two reasons why most people find building new habits hard, this chapter will take you through how you can turn your journaling project into a lifelong habit.

WHY PEOPLE FAIL AT JOURNALING

Besides the complaint that there is just not enough time to add journaling to your regular activities, there is something else that makes people fail at journaling—a type of self-sabotage. Essentially, people set themselves up for failure from the outset unknowingly by having their expectations too high.

For example—and this should not come as a surprise—purchasing one of those crisp, beautiful, designer journals could dramatically increase the pressure to be perfect and possibly inhibit your writing.

You are thinking, "This beautiful journal should be filled with poetic writing, travel adventures, unique experiences recorded in flawless handwriting." In reality, this rarely happens. Journaling is not about glamor. Trying to live up to that expectation will make it an uphill battle. Why not try a regular composition notebook and add decorations as you go, if you wish.

Another common cause of getting disoriented with journaling is expecting to write every day. Again, let me reiterate the fact that there is no correct way of keeping a journal. Some people could be perfectly at home with writing every day, while others could find it too tiring. That's why I say that you should write when and how you want. If you feel journaling daily has been time-consuming or left you uninspired, create your own intervals. Maybe once or twice weekly?

By all means, try to avoid the feeling that it is a chore that you must do. Came home tired and you just want to jump into bed? Yeah, do it. You can write in the morning. If you force yourself, you will soon start detesting it. However, keep yourself accountable by having a sort of personal rulebook that helps you continue journaling regularly, e.g., "If I miss one biweekly entry, I will complete it before the end of the week." Some flexibility but don't fall completely off the wagon because it might be hard to start again.

DISILLUSIONMENT—"WHAT'S THE POINT?"

At the beginning, while making the decision to start a journal, you may encounter discouragement from different areas on whether it will serve its purpose. Disillusionment is formally described as disappointment from learning that something is not what you initially believed it to be.

You might start asking yourself the following questions:

- *"What's the point of putting my thoughts down regularly?"*
- *"Do I even want to read back my thoughts later?"*
- *"I don't want to look back to my younger years!"*

When you first start a new thing, there is often a buzz of excitement and extra energy that you have to commit to it.

You might also have great expectations for where it will go. I call this the "stationery for school" feeling from the buildup of anticipation of a new school year, getting new equipment and clothes (especially stationery!). You might have gone through something similar when getting ready to start journaling. However, as you have gone on, it is no longer new and exciting—it instead starts to feel like something else. It might get boring or even make you feel a little bit worse than you did before. This is perfectly natural.

Daryl Connor calls my "stationery for school" feeling "uninformed optimism." He originally wrote about the emotional cycles of change in the 70s with his colleague Don Kelley and is still helping people make changes in their lives today. Once you get more information on what you are doing, you move to a stage called "informed pessimism" where you start to see some of how much hard work this new endeavor is going to be. There will be a low point before you can then start feeling better about your new habit. Here in what they call "the valley of despair," some people might easily choose to quit their new habit.

At this point it is very important to hold onto your "why," the reason you started journaling in the first place. Things will get better if you keep practicing your habit. You will eventually move up into "informed optimism" where you can start to see your new habit bearing fruit and it feels like less energy each time to do it. The ultimate end point according to Kelley and Connor is "success and fulfillment," which might sound like a lot to promise but consider this a stage where you are journaling regularly and benefiting from it in some new way. It feels easier, more automatic and you are getting more benefits from it than you are expending extra energy on it. Your work has paid off.

Another related hurdle to creating space for journaling is our present-day preference for instant gratification—a lot of us today want results right here and right now, not later on in the journey. So if other things such as inspirational Instagram posts or say, comfort foods, give you the desired rewards right away, they may feel more urgent and worthy of your time and journaling takes a back seat.

Journaling is very unlikely to instantly reward you. The satisfaction comes over time, and is even less apparent to the non-starter who feels too busy to cultivate a new habit. It doesn't have to take too much time to see its usefulness if you define your goals and practice using the ideas presented in Chapters 4 through 7 before fully committing.

Positive gradual changes in resilience, decision making and clarity of mind are some of the perks that journaling might deliver. Instead of focusing on what journaling should not be for you, think about how it can be of use to you and start small. Once you start putting thoughts on paper, you are spurring your brain to get things in motion.

If you are clear about your issues and goals from the onset, there is a good chance that you will start seeing results over time. Journaling will not provide you with immediate change, but the fruits of your efforts will not take long to surface.

> *"Journaling in college took on more significance in my life . . . I was making a whole host of life-changing decisions: What should I major in? Should I go to law school? I also discovered the idea of using your journal as a self-improvement tool."*
>
> — BRETT MCKAY, FOUNDER, THE

ART OF MANLINESS (MCKAY & MCKAY 2020)

THE STRUCTURE OF HABITS

Our routines can help us build structure into our lives and develop a sense of accomplishment in the midst of life's chaos and uncertainty. However, turning our routines into habits is an even bigger step. To be able to create a new habit, you need to understand how habits are structured.

Habits are made of the following three components, which together make up what is referred to as the "habit loop."

HABIT CUES

The first component of the habit loop is events or cues that our subconscious mind has associated with the habit. Whenever we encounter a habit cue, we automatically get the urge to perform the habit. Habit cues come in five forms:

Time: This is one of the most common habit cues. Think of your morning habits; once you wake up you'll most likely go to the bathroom, brush your teeth, take a shower, make breakfast, get dressed, and so on—all purely based on time. Sometimes, it can be even more subtle. You may notice you get a snack or a coffee at exactly the same time in the mid-mornings or your smoke breaks follow a certain time schedule.

For bad habits, finding the reason why they happen at specific times of the day can help you replace them with good ones. For good habits, assigning them specific times can reinforce them. Just like the smoke break could come naturally to someone during the 11 a.m. break, so could making entries to your gratitude journal at 11 p.m.

Location: You might not be thinking about it, but your environment can motivate you to do something. For example, finding a plate of cookies on the kitchen counter could cause you to take a bite. Our habits and behaviors can easily be said to be responses to what surrounds us.

Take, for instance, the famous study on the location of sodas and water at a hospital cafeteria. After adding more water in the vicinity of the cash machines over a six-month period, the sale of water increased by over 25% and that of sodas reduced by over 11%.

Researchers conclude that we will often make purchases not because of what they are but because of *where* they are (Thorndike, 2012).

To form new habits, many studies show that new locations are very effective. This is because we tend to have assigned habits to familiar locations mentally. So, if you want to start a new habit, choosing a specific spot for the habit you want to grow and sticking to it can significantly help you cultivate the habit. Think of what a dedicated smoking zone on campus does for smokers. This is one of the reasons why you might try and create a journaling sanctuary as we outlined in Chapter 3.

Preceding Events: Things that happen in your life can encourage responses that become habits. A phone buzz or social media notification bar lighting up, for example, will typically make you check your phone. The buzz or notification is an example of a preceding event.

When trying to build new habits, preceding events can be very useful. Just link your habit to an event that regularly happens in your day and you can literally keep up with any habit you truly want to keep.

For example, you could say, "As my morning coffee is brewing, I counter check my to-do list to get ready for the day." Or, "Once I am done with dinner, I write down two things I am grateful for." This way, every time you finish dinner, your mind will automatically want to grab the gratitude journal.

Emotions: Often, emotional states have been cues for bad habits. An example is eating when stressed, or shopping online when bored. To build good habits with emotional cues, you have to be aware of what you are feeling. So paying attention to your emotions is a big part of your success in coming up with and maintaining a healthy habit. Could you journal instead when you feel a certain emotion?

Feeling tense and stressed? Maybe try jotting down all the whirring thoughts to slow them down. Getting confused about an idea you want to pitch? Take a few minutes and write it down, flesh it out and boost your confidence. Struggling to make a big decision? Make a table of pros and cons, and add alternatives too. You can look at it with a fresh mind later and stand a better chance of making the right choice.

People Around You: You will certainly have come across quotes like "You are the sum total of the people you meet and interact with," or "You are the average of the 5 people you spend the most time with," and the more popular "Show me your friends and I will tell you who you are." These quotes illustrate the significant influence of the people around you on your habits, behaviors and goals.

To show how much influence your social circle can have on you, consider a study published by the New England Journal of Medicine that found if a friend of yours becomes obese, your risk of becoming obese too increases by an incredible 57%, whether your friend lives blocks away or hundreds of miles from you (Christakis & Fowler, 2007).

Closer to home, you might not drink alcohol regularly, but every time you go out with friends, you end up having a few. Why is that? Definitely because of the people around you. To use this cue to your advantage, surround yourself with those who have the habits that you want to build for yourself.

From the above examples, you can try to identify the best kind of cues that you can use to always remind yourself to journal. For instance, you could set reminders, join a journaling club at school, or create a sanctuary?

THE ACTION

This is the second component of a habit. This is where the actual action takes place in the habit loop. The cues discussed above will be the anchor points within which these actions come to life. The action could be smoking a cigarette, munching on some chocolate, taking a morning run or writing in your gratitude journal.

This part of the loop is the journaling you do in response to your chosen cue(s) that leads to a reward at the end (next section). Without the action (journaling), the habit loop is broken.

We have done a lot of work already on ways of removing barriers to getting started and taking the appropriate actions for your target habit of journaling. For instance, if you were finding having to wait until you get home in the evening breaks your habit loop, you could carry a pocket-size journal. We have just not described it in this way before.

THE REWARD

This is the final component of the habit loop. A reward is the good feeling your brain gets after taking action to fulfill your urges about a certain activity. Depending on the action, the reward will come in many forms—the nicotine buzz after smoking, a feel-good from eating chocolate, relief from a morning run, calmness after bedside journaling, and so on.

The reward is what keeps the habit loop going. If you do not get the reward you hoped for, you will have little reason to keep up the habit. You will get bored and tired soon enough.

To reinforce a new habit, you can give yourself a motivating reward after completing the action. For instance, you could give yourself a cup of hot chocolate once you're done journaling.

That is the structure of a habit. Once you understand this, you can figure out how to use the structure to build and maintain a new habit as well as end a harmful one. You can align the habit you want with the cues that make it easy to achieve, choose routines that support it, and define rewards that will encourage you to continue.

UNREALISTIC GOALS AND EXPECTATIONS

The second biggest impediment to building and maintaining a new habit is trying to achieve too much, too soon. Like I said earlier, this is surely setting yourself up for failure. Since it's a new habit, it will definitely take time to stick. So by all means, take it slow.

Here are tips on how to take things slow;

- **Make Your Goals So Small That You Can't Fail**:

Let it be a gradual progress, rather than a sprint. Trying to change so many things very quickly will wear you down soon enough. As you begin, make it so achievable that you cannot say no. For a daily journal, target one or two lines a day. For fitness, 10 pushups a day is fine. Want to read more? One page a day is great. Basically make your desired habit so easy to achieve that it would be impossible to fail, then you can work your way up.

- **Follow the "Never Miss Twice" Rule**: As you begin, and maybe even along the way, you may slip up and skip your routine. That's okay. As we said before, don't beat yourself up for missing it once—and catch up as soon as it makes sense. Then, the next day get right back on track. The frequency of whatever habit you are aspiring to keep may not be daily. However the rule of thumb remains the same. Get back on that horse as soon as possible. If you allow yourself to miss two consecutive instances of your routine, this could become your new normal. Good thing is, if you've made it as easy as possible to do, it should be much easier to keep yourself in check with this rule.
- **Break It Down**: The true results of your efforts come in increments. The compounding effect of little but consistent effort means that in a few months you will register dramatic progress. So keep it reasonable and easy by breaking down your daily targets into even more achievable chunks. For instance, if you want to do 100 push-ups in a day, do them in sets of 10. If you want to journal about your next big project for 30 minutes every day, why not break it into two and write in the morning before work/school and again later after dinner.

Basically, if you create big goals that are composed of small steps, your habit will become even easier to keep.
- **Patience**: They say slow and steady wins the race. This could not be more relevant than when building a new habit. Find a sustainable pace for yourself and don't rush. Remember, everything worthwhile takes time.

So how can we apply these to our journaling project?

USING THESE HABIT IDEAS TO HELP YOUR JOURNALING

Think about what cues can work best for you. Pick a time you want to be journaling. At what time of the day can you have at least 10 minutes to yourself?

Is it immediately after waking up, or just before getting under the covers? In your daily schedule, maybe you have a considerable amount of time for lunch, or your classes end early and you can afford to sit down for a while before the evening commute. If you are a night owl, when do you give yourself a break to relax?

One of the popular routes to finding your cues is looking at your daily events or rituals. You may have some things that you usually do on a daily basis, such as waking up, showering, fixing your breakfast, praying, your commutes, defined lunch and coffee or tea breaks, and so on. Figure out when it would be easiest to fit your journaling habit without interfering with your daily routine.

The other cue is location. We talked about creating a journaling sanctuary—a place where you feel at peace, alone and safe to pour your heart out. Create it from scratch or identify an already existing place that can give you that peace of mind you need to unload your mind. It might already have the perfect ambience, say by the seaside if you like, but you can also create it.

Manipulate the lighting, scents and sounds to your liking and own it. Ideally, it should be easily accessible to you. It could be a quiet place on campus, your bedroom or a spare room in the house. Do you want to keep the journal there so every time you see it you remember to keep your project alive? Or do you want to always have it with you and take advantage of a temporary sanctuary? Maybe a nice quiet coffee shop or a park could do. The idea is that it should make you feel "It's time to journal!"

Your actions can also be married into your daily routine. Are you artsy? Is drawing, doodling, and sketching how best you express your thoughts? Then draw away. If you are normally expressive, feel free to write down as many paragraphs without restraint. If audio is your thing, record your thoughts into an audio journal even. If you would rather be brief, jot down what you need to in shorthand. By all means, do not let the journaling process be in conflict with your normal, everyday self.

When you are done, you can reward yourself with anything you love doing. Whether that is playing a video game or listening to a song you like, adding a reward to your journaling can help you maintain the already pleasurable habit. It can help you look forward to writing in your journal.

For best effect, ensure the rewards are pleasurable. For instance, don't say, "After writing I will have dinner," which you would have had anyway. Financial rewards are also not recommended, although it depends on how it makes you feel. Keep your rewards simple and small. Basically, let them fit the effort, for example we spoke before about making a cup of hot chocolate.

You could skip ahead slightly and have that cup of hot chocolate while you are journaling and it would work as a reward just the same. Making your journaling sanctuary as enjoyable as possible to write in will reward you every time and help you to build up your habit. You will eventually start to look forward to it. Some people might find that journaling is or becomes a reward in itself if it leaves them feeling calmer, happier or perhaps less confused each time.

Repeat your journaling sequence daily until your brain gets used to it. For example, always record your to-do list or gratitude journal after the last lecture each day, and then have a chocolate bar, grab a latte, or skype chat a friend (or whatever your reward is) before leaving for home.

As you get used to journaling, you can increase your actions, but do it very gradually. Maybe you have found more prompts you want to add to your daily template, or you want to add sleep or worry journaling into your routine (see Chapter 8). Allow yourself to get comfortable with the additions and keep it as enjoyable and sustainable as can be.

In this chapter we have encouraged you to reflect on how your journaling is going after a few weeks or months and consider how you can use ideas around habit forming to help with the next steps in your journey.

10

NEXT STEPS

"Of all the things that have been helpful to me in personal growth and goal achievement, using my journal daily is at the foundation."

— BENJAMIN HARDY, PH.D.

There you go. That is our introduction to journaling. You are now all set to make your journaling project a successful habit for years to come.

Perhaps the most useful answer we can give to the question, *"What is the goal of journaling?"* is the ability to help you achieve the goals you have set for yourself in life. A journal is a personal discipline tool that you can deploy to whatever use you desire. You can make journaling whatever it needs to be for you, so do not let anyone dictate for you what journaling is or is not, or discourage you by suggesting that you are journaling wrong in some way.

Below, let's go through a recap of everything you have learned in this book.

In Chapter 1, we introduced you to the concept of journaling. We saw what you stand to gain by adopting this habit and how you can get started. Starting journaling is as easy as grabbing the nearest blank notebook and letting your most intimate thoughts flow on paper. We also shared with you testimonials of some journalers to give you some inspiration.

In Chapter 2, we looked at the equipment that you need in your journaling journey. We covered the different aspects of your journaling equipment that can make your journaling experience worthwhile. Is it the colors, the texture, or the quality of paper that will make your journaling experience?

We gave you tips on how to identify all the different types of pens, paper and journal types. We also looked at other accessories you might need, including the pen or pencil bag, watercolors, paint brushes, washi tape, sticky notes, and so on. We explored all options at your disposal that can make your journaling experience as well-rounded as it can be.

In Chapter 3, we talked about journaling as a private affair, and shared with you ways to keep your journaling experience personal. These include keeping your journal safe from prying eyes, as well as carving out a safe space for yourself so that you feel that you can be vulnerable when asking yourself potentially difficult questions. And as we say, *Journaling Is For Everyone*, so we gave you many options so that you can find ideas that fit your personality.

In Chapter 4, we answered the most common question for beginners: *Where Do I Start?* As a beginner, you don't have to worry too much about what to write. Instead, you should write *anything* that comes to your mind. We gave you a first exercise to try out and went through some common blocks to starting.

Everyone who's new to journaling will get to a point where they ask themselves if they will be able to create enough time for this new thing in their lives. In Chapter 5, we emphasized the need to first carve out space in your schedule before adding journaling into it. We went on to share options that make it virtually impossible for you to say that you do not have time to journal. We gave you tips on how to blend journaling into your daily routine and made it clear that journaling does not have to require a great deal of time commitment if you do not want it to.

After considering where to position journaling in your daily or weekly routine, Chapter 6 guided you through your first week of trying out journaling regularly. We presented more detailed ideas about how you might journal and what you might use your journaling for.

We looked at how uplifting *writing for yourself* can be and the unique human ability to reflect on our experiences. It's all about the exciting process of self-discovery, where you begin molding your daily life, feelings, emotions and opinions into a higher quality life experience. The chapter concluded by offering you a review of your first week and an opportunity to carry on at this level for a few weeks in order to decide what is working for you.

Chapter 7 expanded upon what you already learned in Chapter 6. The chapter is loaded with tips on the multiple ways you can ensure that you have something exciting and meaningful to write about every day and keep your journaling habit alive.

It introduced the concept of authenticity—a critical ingredient to your journaling project and the potentially very desirable pursuit of gratitude. These ideas can be used to deepen your journaling work. You might have found that the more practical ways of working with goal setting and decision making were more your thing. At the end, we invited you to schedule a special review session with yourself following this longer period of journaling.

Chapter 8 looked at one of perhaps the most hidden hurdles to self-development—a cluttered mind. We traced the reasons behind what many would call a *busy mind* and explored a number of ways that you can relieve yourself from this situation that often leads to clouded judgement and ill-informed decision-making.

We specifically looked at the important role that sleep plays in keeping us healthy and how you can use journaling to blitz busy thoughts that are preventing you from sleeping, before finishing the chapter looking at ways to perhaps put some of your thoughts to sleep themselves by accepting them.

Finally, in Chapter 9, we took a deep dive into habit formation. We looked at how you can build and maintain new habits in your life. Once you have learned all you need as someone who's getting started with journaling, this chapter is probably the most significant. This is because what you learned in this chapter will be very important in helping you remain consistent in your journaling voyage.

This brings us to the tail end of this beginner guide to journaling. We hope you enjoyed it and are ready to continue with this exciting and fulfilling habit. We would be especially grateful if you could take the time to leave us a review of your experience with this book—for the platform on which you purchased it.

As you already know, this guide is the first in our *Journaling Is For Everyone* series. We have more guides coming up in the series. There is much more to know beyond this introductory guide, and we will be bringing you more books to help you with your future steps. These will include a great deal more in-depth exercises to help you with self-discovery.

In addition, we will be diving deeper into topics such as sleep, journaling with the seasons, decision making, gratitude, acceptance and authenticity.

If there are particular topics that you are interested in, then please do let us know as we love to hear from our readers. Email us at jessmaple@robinroundpress.com and we will be releasing the most sought-after book next. We will listen if you speak!

APPENDIX

If you feel you are in need of more structured support in the form of counseling, or you are in a crisis, please find below some options that you might find useful to consider.

1. For immediate help in a crisis or if you know someone is in immediate danger **CALL 911** or go to the nearest emergency room.
2. National Suicide Prevention Lifeline: Call 1-800-273-8255; En Español 1-888-628-9454. This is a free and confidential crisis hotline available 24 hours a day, every day. It connects you to the nearest crisis center on the Lifeline national network. The centers provide mental health referrals and crisis counseling. If you are deaf, have hearing loss or hard of hearing, contact the Lifeline through TTY on 1-800-799-4889.
3. The Crisis Text Line: **Text HELLO to 741741**. This a 24/7 service that serves anyone during any type of a crisis. It helps connect you with a counselor who can give you the support and information you need.

4. Veterans Crisis Line: **Call 1-800-273-8255 and press 1 or text to 838255.** This is also a free and confidential service that connects veterans to trained responders. It is available 24/7 to all veterans. If you are hard of hearing, deaf, or have hearing loss, call 1-800-799-4889.
5. Disaster Distress Helpline: **Call 1-800-985-5990 or text "TalkWithUs" to 6674.** This 24/7 service provides immediate crisis counseling for anyone under emotional stress from human-caused or natural disasters. It is free, confidential and multilingual.
6. **Your Primary Care Provider:** They are an important resource that can help with diagnosis and referrals to specialists.

FEDERAL RESOURCES

1. Substance Abuse and Mental Health Services Administration (SAMHSA): You can get general mental health information and help locating treatment services near you by calling the **SAMHSA Treatment Referral Helpline at 1-800-662-HELP (4357)**. You can also use the Behavioural Health Treatment Locator.
2. Health Resources and Services Administration (HRSA): The website has information on finding healthcare that is affordable as well as centers offering care on a sliding fee scale.
3. Centers for Medicare & Medicaid Services (CMS): The website contains information on eligibility and benefits for mental health programs and how to enroll.

4. The National Library of Medicine (NLM) MedlinePlus: Find directories and the list of organizations that help you identify health practitioners here.
5. Mental Health and Addiction Insurance Help: Find resources on your questions about insurance coverage for mental health care here.

OTHER RESOURCES

1. **State and county agencies:** Your state or county websites should have information on health services in your area.
2. **Your Insurance Provider:** A representative from your insurance provider should be aware of local healthcare providers you can visit under your plan. You can also search through their website.
3. **University, College or Medical Schools:** Your institution may offer you treatment options. You can search for this information on their website or visit the related department.

REFERENCES

Achebe, C. (1994). *No Longer at Ease* (Reprint ed.). Penguin Books.

1 in 3 adults don't get enough sleep. (2016, Feb 18). CDC. https://www.cdc.gov/media/releases/2016/p0215-enough-sleep.html.

Baer, D. (2013, Oct 7). To Make Better Decisions, Map Them Out. Fast Company. https://www.fastcompany.com/3013975/to-make-better-decisions-map-them-out

Baikie, K., & Wilhelm, K. (2005). Emotional and physical health benefits of expressive writing. *Advances in Psychiatric Treatment*, 11(5), 338-346. doi:10.1192/apt.11.5.338.

Berninger, V. W., Abbott, R. D., Jones, J., Wolf, B. J., Gould, L., Anderson-Youngstrom, M., Shimada, S., & Apel, K. (2006). Early development of language by hand: composing, reading, listening, and speaking connections; three letter-writing modes; and fast mapping in spelling. *Developmental Neuropsychology*, 29(1), 61–92. https://doi.org/10.1207/s15326942dn2901_5.

Cardone, G. (n.d.). Write Your Goals Down Again Before You Go to Sleep. GrantCardone.com. https://grantcardone.com/write-your-goals-down-again-before-you-go-to-sleep/

Christakis, N. A., & Fowler, J. H. (2007). The spread of obesity in a large social network over 32 years. *The New England journal of medicine*, 357(4), 370–379. https://doi.org/10.1056/NEJMsa066082.

Clear, J. (n.d). How To Start New Habits That Actually Stick. Jamesclear.com. https://jamesclear.com/three-steps-habit-change

Collins, B. (2018, May 16). How To Start A Journaling Habit Today. Better Humans. https://medium.com/better-humans/how-to-start-a-journaling-habit-today-99d5f98fe8cc

Color Psychology: The Emotional Effects of Colors. (n.d.) Art Therapy Blog. http://www.arttherapyblog.com/online/color-psychology-psychologica-effects-of-colors/#.YBPbsegzbIU

Drowsy Driving (n.d.). CDC. https://www.cdc.gov/sleep/about_sleep/drowsy_driving.html#:~:text=Being%20awake%20for%20at%20least%2024%20hours%20is%20equal%20to,%25%20BAC)%20in%20all%20states.

Frank, Anne. *The Diary of a Young Girl*. Translated by B. M. Mooyaart-Doubleday. Contact Publishing. 1952.

Gardner, S. & Albee, D. (2015). Study focuses on strategies for achieving goals, resolutions. Press Releases. 266. https://scholar.dominican.edu/news-releases/266

Get Enough Sleep (n.d). ODPHP. https://health.gov/myhealthfinder/topics/everyday-healthy-living/mental-health-and-relationships/get-enough-sleep#:~:text=Stay%20at%20a%20healthy%20weight,in%20school%20and%20at%20work

Google Books Ngram Viewer – Google Product. (n.d.). https://books.google.com/ngrams/graph?content=diary%2C+journal&year_start=1800&year_end=2019&corpus=26&smoothing=3&direct_url=t1%3B%2Cdiary%3B%2Cc0%3B.t1%3B%2Cjournal%3B%2Cc0#t1%3B%2Cdiary%3B%2Cc0%3B.t1%3B%2Cjournal%3B%2Cc0

Hardy, B. (2017, Sep 23). Writing In A Journal Has Helped Me Create My Future And Achieve My Goals. Inc.com. https://www.inc.com/benjamin-p-hardy/how-i-use-my-journal-to-create-my-future-achieve-my-goals.html

Hardy, B. (2019, Nov 21). Keeping A Daily Journal Could Change Your Life. Inc.com. https://www.inc.com/benjamin-p-hardy/why-keeping-a-daily-journal-could-change-your-life.html

Harteneck, P. (2016, April 8). 5 Ways to Stop Your Racing Thoughts. Psychology Today.

https://www.psychologytoday.com/us/blog/women-s-mental-health-matters/201604/5-ways-stop-your-racing-thoughts

Işık, Ş., Ergüner-Tekinalp, B. The Effects of Gratitude Journaling on Turkish First Year College Students' College Adjustment, Life Satisfaction and Positive Affect. *International Journal for the Advancement of Counselling,* 39, 164–175 (2017). https://doi.org/10.1007/s10447-017-9289-8.

Kelley and Conner's Emotional Cycle of Change: Keeping Going When You Make a Voluntary Change. (n.d.). Retrieved from https://www.mindtools.com/pages/article/kelley-conner-cycle.htm

Leslie, M. (2017, Aug 15). Five-day fasting diet could fight disease, slow aging. *Science.* https://www.sciencemag.org/news/2017/02/five-day-fasting-diet-could-fight-disease-slow-aging.

Lindberg, S. (2018, Nov 27). 5 Ways Accepting Your Anxiety Can Make You More Powerful. Healthline.org. https://www.healthline.com/health/how-anxiety-can-make-you-more-powerful#1.-Anxiety-acts-as-a-protective-mechanism

Luders, E., Kurth, F., Mayer, E. A., Toga, A. W., Narr, K. L., & Gaser, C. (2012). The unique brain anatomy of meditation practitioners: alterations in cortical gyrification. *Frontiers in Human Neuroscience,* 6(34). https://doi.org/10.3389/fnhum.2012.00034.

Martineau, S. (2015, Feb 24). A Mantra for Habit Building: Never Miss Twice. Medium.com. https://medium.com/undieting-collection/a-mantra-for-habit-building-never-miss-twice-3950b3132223#:~:text=Never%20miss%20twice%20takes%20pressure,desires%20from%20time%20to%20time.

McDonald, J. (2019, July 26). When Are Heartbeats Audible During Pregnancy? FactCheck.org. https://www.factcheck.org/2019/07/when-are-heartbeats-audible-during-pregnancy/

McKay, B. & McKay, K. (2020, Sep 7). Why I Stopped Journaling.

The Art of Manliness.
https://www.artofmanliness.com/articles/why-i-stopped-journaling/

Miller R. W. (2017, Aug 20). Here's Why Teens Keep Diaries. *BuzzFeed*. https://www.buzzfeed.com/rachelwmiller/teens-on-why-they-keep-a-diary.

Plato, Fowler, H. N., Lamb, W. R. M., Bury, R. G., & Shorey, P. (1914). Plato in twelve volumes: With an English translation. London: W. Heinemann.

Scullin, M. K., Krueger, M. L., Ballard, H. K., Pruett, N., & Bliwise, D. L. (2018). The effects of bedtime writing on difficulty falling asleep: A polysomnographic study comparing to-do lists and completed activity lists. *Journal of Experimental Psychology: General*, 147(1), 139–146. https://doi.org/10.1037/xge0000374.

Simmons, M. (2017, Aug 17). I spent years discovering the simple tactics gurus like Oprah, Einstein, and Buffett used to become successful—here they are. Quartz. https://qz.com/1054094/i-spent-years-discovering-the-simple-tactics-gurus-like-oprah-einstein-and-buffett-used-to-become-successful-here-they-are/

Sleep deprivation is torture: Amnesty. (2006, Oct 3). The Sydney Morning Herald (SMH). https://www.smh.com.au/national/sleep-deprivation-is-torture-amnesty-20061004-gdoiq8.html.

Thorndike, A.N., Sonnenberg, L, Riis, J., Barraclough, S,. & Levy, D. E. (2012). A 2-Phase Labeling and Choice Architecture Intervention to Improve Healthy Food and Beverage Choices. *American Journal of Public Health*. 102(3). https://doi:10.2105/ajph.2011.300391.

Top 31 Most Inspiring Quotes About Journaling. (2020, January 22). https://www.unicothings.com/quotes-about-journaling/

White, R. (2017, May 25). Inside Roald Dahl's Writing Hut. RoaldDahl.com. https://www.roalddahl.com/blog/2017/may/inside-roald-dahls-writing-hut

Printed in Great Britain
by Amazon